Blessed Are the Poor in Spirit

Reflections on the Beatitudes

Sabatino Majorano

ST. PAUL BOOKS & MEDIA

Nihil Obstat:
    Very Rev. Timothy J. Shea, V.F.

Imprimatur:
    ✠Bernard Cardinal Law

May 10, 1995

The Scripture quotations contained herein are from the *Revised Standard Version Bible with the Apocrypha/Deuterocanonical Books,* copyrighted © 1973 by the Division of Christian Education of the National Council of Churches of Christ in the U.S.A., and are used by permission. All rights reserved.

Photo credits: FSP 15, 59, 87; Mary Emmanuel Alves, FSP 43, 77; Colleen Lamkins 70
Design by Mary Joseph Peterson, FSP

ISBN: 0-8198-1147-5

Original title: *Beati...Beati...*
Original series title: *Note sulle "dieci parole"/"beatitudini"*
Copyright © 1991, Figlie di San Paolo, Milan, Italy
Translated from the Italian by Anne Eileen Heffernan, FSP and Mary Lea Hill, FSP

English edition copyright © 1995, Daughters of St. Paul

Printed and published in the U.S.A. by Pauline Books & Media, 50 St. Paul's Avenue, Boston, MA 02130.

Pauline Books & Media is the publishing house of the Daughters of St. Paul, an international congregation of women religious serving the Church with the communications media.

1 2 3 4 5   99 98 97 96 95

CONTENTS

Introduction 4

The Beatitudes 6

Overview of *Blessed Are the Poor in Spirit* 9

From the Commandments to the Beatitudes 10

Blessed Are the Poor 18

Blessed Are Those Who Mourn 26

Blessed Are the Meek 33

Blessed Are Those Who Hunger
and Thirst for Justice 41

Blessed Are the Merciful 49

Blessed Are the Pure of Heart 57

Blessed Are the Peacemakers 66

Blessed Are the Persecuted 74

Let's Celebrate the Lord Our God 82

Witness—The Message of Francis of Assisi 84

Notes 89

About the Author 93

About this Series 93

INTRODUCTION

"What values has Christ brought into the world by saving it? Especially, those of the beatitudes, which constitute the law of the kingdom (cf. Mt 5:1-2). These can seem paradoxical, but they renew all of human behavior....

"A man or woman who lives according to the beatitudes, who knows their absolute value, has found a treasure. In fact, he or she becomes a treasure for the world. This person announces Paradise. Ask yourselves: how can we contribute right now to religion in the year 2000? Won't it be wonderful if today's young adults pledge themselves to undertake this journey fearlessly? Everything is possible with the breath that comes from Jesus, the breath of his Spirit. Behold the love that comes from God."[1]

The following pages are dictated by these perspectives, which are fundamental for every believer. The purpose of this booklet is to help the reader enter with deeper understanding into the beatitudes, as a journey of authenticity, love and hope.

This won't be an exegesis of the biblical text, even though a number of studies have been consulted. The main thrust will be to project the beatitudes into everyday life. Indicating some areas as particularly fundamental, these chapters can help make the topics concrete and meaningful, even for persons who don't recognize their validity. The purpose is to open the reader to the beatitudes' sense of paradox, but above all, to show that the beatitudes form each of us into a sign of the new hope that Christ has infused into the history of each person and of all humanity.

Our journey begins with reflection on the meaning and role of the beatitudes in the Christian life. We will then analyze each beatitude, following the order presented in the Gospel of Matthew.

The many biblical references are meant to be an invitation to meditate personally or in groups on at least some of these passages. The same goes for the texts of the Church's magisterium, beginning with those of Vatican II: they are offered as an invitation to grow in a freedom that is nourished by a true sense of belonging to the Church.

The following pages are especially meant to stimulate the reader to project the light of the beatitudes on to the lifestyles most common today, so that all may search together for ways to incarnate into these the new hope that is the risen Christ.

Sabatino Majorano, C.Ss.R.

The Beatitudes

From the Gospel of Matthew (5:3-10)

Blessed are the poor in spirit,
    for theirs is the kingdom of heaven.

Blessed are those who mourn,
    for they shall be comforted.

Blessed are the meek,
    for they shall inherit the earth.

Blessed are those who hunger and thirst for righteousness,
    for they shall be satisfied.

Blessed are the merciful,
    for they shall obtain mercy.

Blessed are the pure of heart,
    for they shall see God.

Blessed are the peacemakers,
    for they shall be called sons of God.

Blessed are those who are persecuted for righteousness' sake,
    for theirs is the kingdom of heaven.

From the Gospel of Luke (6:20-22)

Blessed are you poor,
  for yours is the kingdom of God.
Blessed are you that hunger now,
  for you shall be satisfied.
Blessed are you that weep now,
  for you shall laugh.
Blessed are you when men hate you,
  and when they exclude you and revile you,
  and cast out your name as evil,
  on account of the Son of man!

Overview

Blessed Are the Poor in Spirit

This booklet introduces reflection on the beatitudes by proposing that the meaning of the moral dimension of human beings is freedom. In practice, freedom realizes itself as love that builds up life for those who live the beatitudes and for others, permitting them to enter into symbiotis with the truth.

When moral reflection does not reveal the call to freedom and life, it cannot engage our interest, and when God himself is reduced to being the guardian of imperative moral limits, it seems legitimate to disown him and relegate him to the margins of life so we can affirm our freedom.

Considering the importance of the heart as a person's internal decision-making center at the level of values, and seeing the moral life as gift, call and participation, we are invited to look at the journey marked out by the beatitudes as the foundation of the commitment to the good which is the vocation of every human person.

—The author, therefore, presents each of the beatitudes in the broad outlines of the Gospel's requirements for the kingdom.

—The abundant considerations that the author offers for each beatitude are followed by a plan for reflection.

—Then the reader is invited to pray with a canticle of Francis of Assisi and to reflect on the witness of the saint's life, seen in the full light of the beatitudes.

From the Commandments to the Beatitudes

Moral norms are still regarded with considerable suspicion and uneasiness, even though we're becoming aware of a new need for them. The challenges and problems that we find ourselves facing today, which concern the very survival of the human race, call for responsibility and courageous choices on the part of everyone. We haven't yet succeeded in shaking off the fear that behind their beautiful wording, moral norms and laws conceal an attempt to restrict human freedom.

I always remember what a young woman said at the beginning of the celebration of Reconciliation: "I don't want to be here, because I'm afraid that what we're going to do will ask me to stop living fully. But I want to live fully! I want nothing more than to live fully till the end of my life!"

Too often moral reflections, even on fundamental aspects of life, can't manage to avoid this blockage, whether in the language used or in the way the argument is presented. Thus, such reflection becomes incapable of really interesting us. Even faith itself resents it: when God is reduced to the status of a guardian of imperative moral limits, it seems legitimate to disown him or relegate him to the margins of life so one can affirm one's freedom.

In the Gospel the sense of all the moral norms is one of life, of fullness, of happiness. Christ forcefully proclaims: "I came that they may have life, and have it abundantly" (Jn 10:10). With his death and resurrection, he radically defeated every form of death, becoming for each of us "a life-giving spirit" (1 Cor 15:45). He makes himself bread of eternal life, inviting us to share this bread unceasingly in love (cf. Jn 6:57-58).

Therefore the apostle Paul could decisively remind the Galatians: "For freedom Christ has set us free; stand fast therefore, and do not submit again to a yoke of slavery" (Gal 5:1). But with the same vigor he also reminded them that not all liberty is really such, but only that which bears the quality of love: "For you were called to freedom, brethren; only do not use your freedom as an opportunity for the flesh, but through love be servants of one another" (Gal 5:13).

To make liberty really actualize itself as love that builds up life for ourselves and others—this is the ultimate meaning of the moral dimension. Freedom then enters into symbiosis with the truth: it grounds itself in the truth, avoiding the risk of depreciating itself in arbitrariness or in illusion, which for the believer has the face of sin.

Morality is a journey of life, of love, of liberty. The beatitudes are meant not only to recall us to this fundamental significance, but to help us to discern the steps that we can take in the various situations of every day.

The heart

Matthew's Gospel gives particular emphasis to the sermon on the mount. We quickly note the parallelism—although dense with newness—between this discourse and the promulgation of the law on Sinai (cf. Ex 19-20). It seems clear that from the beginning the Christian community sensed that the beatitudes were to be the fundamental criteria for life: they were to mark out the way of a new justice, not opposed to that of Israel, but related to it in the sense of fullness and completion: "Think not that I have come to abolish the law and the prophets; I have come not to abolish them but to fulfill them" (Mt 5:17).

This completion emphasizes the necessity of transcending whatever justice is preoccupied only with acts and behavior, to which should be counterpoised the justice that springs from the heart: "For I tell you, unless your righteousness exceeds that of the scribes and Pharisees, you will never enter the kingdom of heaven" (Mt 5:20).

It is within this context that the eight beatitudes of Matthew are situated. "The accent is placed on the interior dispositions that conform the person to the will of God. Six out of the eight beatitudes are directly related to these dispositions. The two 'active' beatitudes, which concern the merciful and the peacemakers, indicate practices that also manifest dispositions of the heart—those which must inspire the Christian in relationship with his or her neighbor. The remaining six beatitudes largely define the believer's attitude before God."[2]

Luke's version (6:20-22) is set in a different atmosphere, emphasized by the addition of the "woes": "Addressed directly to the disciples, expressed in the second person ('you'), these beatitudes describe them as people who are poor, in contrast with others who are rich, as people who are hungry, as against those who are satisfied, as people who weep, in contrast with others who laugh, and finally, as the objects of all sorts of ill treatment, as against those who are flattered and fawned upon. Clearly, this no longer has to do with spiritual dispositions, but with external, economic and social conditions that are extremely painful."[3]

Taken together, the two versions show that the beatitudes chiefly concern the more specifically spiritual dimensions of our life. But also stressed is the new relationship with God that Christ gives the believer, which entails an obligation to renew history to its depths. The reception of salvation makes each of us a privileged artisan of solidarity and fraternal communion. Faith renders us capable of bearing fruits of life for the whole world and presses us to rise above any discrimination, opposition or injustice.

All this springs from a heart renewed by the presence of the Spirit. It's enough to reread the eighth chapter of the letter to the Romans. Through the gift of the Spirit, Christ has freed us from our powerlessness; now we live in him with the confidence of sons and daughters, discerning the footsteps of goodness in history and experiencing the transformation of our weakness into strength. Our whole life is thus characterized by a profound security that nothing can impair.

Springing from a heart renewed by the Spirit, good is not only experienced as possible, but it again becomes the object of our desire. True, the egotistical desires of the "old man" still remain strong, or more accurately, they are skillfully exploited by the consumer logic of our society. But, it is equally true that in Christ we rediscover the taste for authentic good (cf. Rom 8:5-12; Gal 5:16-23). In fact, we understand that this good corresponds to our fullest and most profound truth and dignity. It becomes beatitude.

The gift

Concretizing the needs of the renewed heart and being desired and recognized by this same heart, moral good is no longer viewed as restricting freedom. Love shows freedom the more authentic way of realizing itself. Not even when love takes the form of a pressing need does it repress freedom; rather, love guarantees freedom, consistency of truth and of meaning.

The Second Vatican Council could therefore affirm: "In the depths of his conscience, man detects a law which he does not impose upon himself, but which holds him to obedience. Always summoning him to love good and to avoid evil, the voice of conscience when necessary speaks to his heart: do this, shun that."[4]

Moral life thus reveals itself first as gift, then as obligation; first as call, then as response; first as participation, then as responsibility. It is life courageously straining ahead toward fullness. It is a marvelous discovery: each of us is a precious talent, entrusted to our own freedom by the Father's love, so as to bear fruit for the good of the entire human race. This talent must be invested with confidence.

When confronted with any challenge on behalf of the good, the believer will remember that this is a call from Christ to participate responsibly in the salvation history of all humanity. Before being a duty, the appeal to do good is a gesture of trust, a potential, a grace. It should be welcomed with gratitude, with the knowledge that Christ shares with us his own strength, which has overcome death. With him we can accomplish even what we would never be able to do on our own.

The Eucharist repeatedly reminds us of this. As "the summit and source" of the whole Christian life, the Eucharist reveals to us not only the horizons and contours of the good, but also its concrete realizations in history. Above all, the Eucharist shows us that everything is grace. From this stems the courage of witness and generous realization.

The beatitudes bring us back to this Eucharistic logic, pointing it out to us as essential to the whole of Christian life. Then we become praise of the Father in fraternal sharing. We discover a profound joy that does not deceive us in the face of the difficulties that are never lacking, but which projects these into the cross of Christ, which has become the fountainhead of life for all.

The journey

In St. Matthew's Gospel, the chapter that contains the beatitudes concludes with the projection of limitless horizons: "You, therefore, must be perfect as your heavenly Father is perfect." Luke specifies: "Be merciful, even as your Father is merciful" (Lk 6:36).

Goodness can never become formalism, nor mechanical repetition of gestures even if they are positive. It is a journey in which one should never pause, because the goal is the very fullness of God. It's like climbing a mountain, where each step opens up new horizons and enkindles the desire to keep going, urging the climber to forget the fatigue already accumulated. And, as in climbing, we travel more securely if we are roped together.

The beatitudes teach us to combine a genuine drive toward the final goal with great care in taking each step, even small, that leads toward it. We need to attentively weigh the concrete situations of our personal story. What is important is to loyally continue on the journey.

"Man, who has been called to live God's wise and loving design in a responsible manner, is an historical being who day by day builds himself up through his many free decisions; and so he knows, loves and accomplishes moral good by stages of growth." It will be necessary "to progress unceasingly." This will be made possible by "a sincere and active desire to gain ever better knowledge of the values enshrined in and fostered by the law of God. [Persons] must also be supported by an upright and generous willingness to embody these values in their concrete decisions."[5]

Indispensable for this journey is profound confidence in the specific plan of the Father for each of us and in the provident care of the Holy Spirit, who reveals and actuates this plan. He has given us many means for discerning his voice: the magisterium of the Church, the signs of the times, the deepening of awareness through conversation and dialogue, the norms delineated by ethical reflection. All these are to be used with fidelity and wisdom.

What the beatitudes are about, then, is a commitment to the good, based on the specific vocation of each person. They enable us to journey together toward the fullness of holiness, valuing the gifts and abilities of all.[6]

For Reflection

"Only in freedom can man direct himself toward goodness. Our contemporaries make much of this freedom and pursue it eagerly; and rightly to be sure. Often however they foster it perversely as a license for doing whatever pleases them, even if it is evil. For its part, authentic freedom is an exceptional sign of the divine image within man."[7] How can we make God known as the origin and horizon of human freedom, not its negation?

"I am the way, and the truth, and the life," responds Christ decisively to the doubts of Thomas (Jn 14:6). Our culture doesn't always make it easy to understand the strict relationship that exists between life, truth and morality; sometimes, in fact, it denies this. But this relationship is essential for a meaningful life.

If not all of this is simple for you, either, be honest with yourself and note when you find it difficult to live the relationship between life, truth and morality. Then speak with your spiritual guide, or with someone else whom you trust, so that he or she may help you grow.

Most often people reduce happiness to an immediate response to experienced needs. But thinking and living in this way, we risk being confined by the manipulations that the various forms of power exercise on these same needs. We must ask ourselves what quality is needed for the attainment of true human happiness. From this perspective the beatitudes suggest a courageous journey.

Blessed Are the Poor

Matthew's Gospel clearly shows that the subjects of this beatitude are the poor in spirit: "Blessed are the poor in spirit, for theirs is the kingdom of heaven" (5:3). Instead, the beatitudes of Luke emphasize poverty in the concrete, balancing it with: "But woe to you that are rich, for you have received your consolation" (6:24).

These two perspectives are closely connected. It makes no sense to contrast spiritual poverty with exterior poverty or to separate the two, as was done in the past and unfortunataely still happens. The beatitude calls us to live both types of poverty constructively, if we want to belong to the kingdom.

A correct relationship with the goods of the earth presupposes that we develop a correct relationship with ourselves—that the sense and purpose of our life be clear. Things invade and possess us, transforming themselves into idols that demand the sacrifice of ourselves and others. When instead we are free from the slavery of possession, then we strongly desire to make a commitment, so that every human being may have everything that is required by his or her dignity as a person.

Creatures and children

Evangelical poverty begins with the recognition that we are creatures, called into existence by an act of love: "Then God said, 'Let us make man in our image, after our likeness; and let them have dominion over the fish of the sea, and over the birds of the air, and over the cattle, and over all the earth, and over every creeping thing that creeps upon the earth.' So God created man in his own image, in the image of God he created him; male and female he created them" (Gen 1:26-27).

None of us can pretend to be an absolute master—neither of our own life nor of the lives of others, be they persons or other living creatures. Life is a gift from God to be cared for and brought to fullness. The more we know this, the closer we draw to the mystery of God. We are his images.

The love of God has gone beyond this, however. In Christ God has made us his children. "For you did not receive the spirit of slavery to fall back into fear," writes the Apostle Paul, "but you have received the spirit of sonship. When we cry, 'Abba! Father!' it is the Spirit himself bearing witness with our spirit that we are children of God, and if children, then heirs, heirs of God and fellow heirs with Christ, provided we suffer with him in order that we may also be glorified with him" (Rom 8:15-17).

Since we receive being and life from God, we can't think that a relationship with God places limits on human dignity. Certainly there are idols. But God offers himself as possibility, ground and fullness of freedom. Our everyday experience confirms this: what does justice become when it rejects any reference to a transcendent absolute? And doesn't love always bear within itself at least a nostalgia for the absolute?

Those who are poor according to the Gospel know that they must hear life's ultimate truth from God. Thanks to Christ, they have become aware that this is a truth of love. They let the Spirit announce it incessantly within the depths of their consciousness: "It is the Spirit himself bearing witness with our spirit that we are children of God" (Rom 8:16). Therefore, they build their life project and their choices on this. They find themselves enriched by the very wealth and power of God.

This does not mean distrusting what is human, but rather finding the roots of human dignity. Then the courage is born to travel the road toward the truth in its entirety, not only for the sake of admiring it, but in order to make it the foundation of personal freedom.

The gospel poor know that life and history have meaning. They decisively commit themselves to seek it, without letting themselves be discouraged by difficulties or ensnared by the sirens that seem so gratifying at first sight but in reality always bind and enslave.

Life, then, is charged with a tension of love. And the poor according to the Gospel accept it as their vocation. That is, they experience life as an appeal that calls them to their responsibility, as a talent to develop with courage, as reciprocity in view of communion. They are not afraid, therefore, to serve others; rather, they are convinced that only love actively committed in reciprocal service is the authentic human face of freedom (cf. Jn 13:14-15).

With his or her sincere availability toward others, the believer witnesses to and proclaims the dignity of the image and child of God that is proper to every human being. No one can wrench this precious treasure away from the believer. Therefore, he or she endeavors to be faithful to this dignity in every choice made.

"Having" at the service of "being"

Those who are poor according to the Gospel find themselves rich in what constitutes true human wealth. They experience a life full of meaning, of communion, of expectation. They are made rich by the self-giving of God in Christ. Truly they have found the treasure that cannot be eaten by moths nor stolen by thieves (cf. Lk 12:33-34).

The kingdom of heaven is theirs—not only in expectation, faithfully waiting for the final return of Christ, but as a reality already begun which tends to completion. The gospel poor have experienced the need to watch over themselves and shun all greed, "for a man's life does not consist in the abundance of his possessions" (Lk 12:15). They energetically testify that true joy can stem only from this true wealth.

Thus they establish a relationship with the goods of the earth that does not make them slaves of "having," but rather illumines them and enables them to keep the meaning of earthly goods always in view. They possess goods in a truly human manner, placing them at the service of themselves and others.

The daily news is clear proof of what earthly goods become when we let ourselves be ruled by egotistical greed for possession. They transform themselves into sources of rivalry, of violence, of death.

The Gospel asks us never to forget that the only human way to possess goods is to share them. The parable of the poor Lazarus is signficant. To the rich man "who was clothed in purple and fine linen and who feasted sumptuously every day," without any sense of solidarity toward the poor Lazarus, "full of sores, who desired to be fed with what fell from the rich man's table," Abraham said: "Son, remember that you in your lifetime recieved your good things, and Lazarus in like manner evil things; but now he is comforted here, and you are in anguish" (cf. Lk 16:19-30).

John Paul II writes that the Christian tradition has never considered the right to ownership "as absolute and untouchable. On the contrary, it has always understood this right within the broader context of the right common to all to use the goods of the whole of creation: the right to private property is subordinated to the right to common use, to the fact that goods are meant for everyone."[8]

All forms of ownership are to be planned and viewed in the light of the universal destination of goods. Courage and creativity are needed to identify ways of living this way in today's complex society.

The gospel poor don't despise earthly goods but love them in the light of their more authentic meaning. They know that goods are signs of the creative love of God. Therefore, they use them with respect, inserting them into the praise that in their freedom they are called to give to God. But they know that goods are also signs and instruments of communion with other human beings, so they possess them in an attitude of sincere solidarity.

Consumerism and luxury are always threats to watch out for. The episode of the rich young man (cf. Lk 18:18-27) is significant. When joint use becomes egotistical possession, goods no longer take into account the call that comes from God. And so we read the bitter consideration of Christ: "How hard it is for those who have riches to enter the kingdom of God! For it is easier for a camel to go through the eye of a needle than for a rich man to enter the kingdom of God" (Lk 18:24-25).

"The evil does not consist in 'having' as such, but in possessing without regard for the quality and the ordered hierarchy of the goods one has."[9]

From the viewpoint of the poor

Someone who is poor according to the Gospel comes to understand the logic with which God works out our salvation. He or she acquires the eyes of Mary, who proclaims in the *Magnificat*: "He has put down the mighty from their thrones, and exalted those of low degree" (Lk 1:52-53). John Paul II comments: "Drawing from Mary's heart, from the depth of her faith expressed in the words of the *Magnificat*, the Church renews ever more effectively in herself the awareness that the truth about the God who saves, the truth about God who is the source of every gift, cannot be separated from the manifestation of his love of preference for the poor and humble."[10]

The reasons for God's preferential choice are many. We will never totally grasp all of them. Certainly they include the poor person's openness to hope, sense of solidarity and greater readiness to accept help. But these facts cannot be absolutized or idealized, since poverty and misery—especially if due to the egoism of others—may simply be sources of bitterness and desperation.

Perhaps the most important reason is that only if we start with those who are in greater need, because they are more scarred by the experience of evil, can we so act that salvation will be granted to all.

Furthermore, in this way we can recognize salvation as love that asks for loving acceptance, not something that can be merited through one's unaided efforts or directly purchased with money.

We need to decisively begin to share with the poor and needy. Solidarity can't remain on the level of words or statements of principles. It must concretize itself in active commitment. The old and new forms of poverty with their burden of human suffering are a warning for us. There must be individual generosity, as well as consistent decisions made at the political and economic levels.

It isn't right to face these problems from the perspective of the strong, the healthy or the wealthy. Though aware that this won't always be understood, the believer will persist in viewing everything through the eyes of the weak, the sick, the small, the poor. This is the only route to true quality of life for all.

The issue is becoming always more urgent because of the dissolution of solidarity that can be noted at all levels. Moreover, some people interpret the events of 1989 as the definitive victory of capitalism. John Paul II states: "We have seen that it is unacceptable to say that the defeat of so-called 'real socialism' leaves capitalism as the only model of economic organization. It is necessary to break down the barriers and monopolies which leave so many countries on the margins of development, and to provide all individuals and nations with the basic conditions which will enable them to share in development. This goal calls for programmed and responsible efforts on the part of the entire international community."[11]

Today, the horizons of the gospel poor are more and more identified with those of the entire world. Today everyone can be questioned energetically about the human value of a well-being that carries suffering and injustice on its shoulders. The face of authentic evangelical poverty is expressed only by a practical solidarity with the needy near and far. It is thus that the kingdom of heaven becomes ours.

For Reflection

"The man of today seems ever to be under threat from what he produces, that is to say from the result of the work of his hands and, even more so, of the work of his intellect and the tendencies of his will."[12] Adequate ethical growth founded on recognition of the truth is indispensable. How can we promote this kind of awareness today?

The glamor of possessing and of consuming permeates our whole cultural context. It's difficult to escape this. Do we keep alive within us a strong critical sense, so as not to be imprisoned by "consumer attitudes and lifestyles...which are objectively improper and often damaging to...physical and spiritual health?"[13]

Blessed Are Those Who Mourn

This is the most paradoxical of the beatitudes. Today, still more than in the past, we have difficulty understanding it. In fact, our society does everything it can to remove anything that signifies suffering or failure. The styles of life that are demanded all emphasize efficiency, success and pleasure.

Yet the gospel statement is clear. Luke renders it even more strongly: "Blessed are you that weep now, for you shall laugh.... Woe to you that laugh now, for you shall mourn and weep" (Lk 6:21, 25).

Is it a consoling viewpoint that leads to relativizing the present and giving it no importance, projecting it into a distant future that inverts its image? Those who make this accusation against Christian hope have never been few. Instead, while hope speaks of the future, it is of a future already begun, entrusted to our responsibility: "She [the Church] further teaches that a hope related to the end of time does not diminish the importance of intervening duties but rather undergirds the acquittal of them with fresh incentives."[14]

The beatitude about those who mourn doesn't imply passive resignation or irresponsibility regarding evil in all its forms. Rather, it stimulates greater realism. We don't conquer evil by clearing it away, hiding it and confusing ourselves. We have to take responsibility for it, give it meaning, identify it and resolve its true causes.

John Paul II reminds us: "Suffering is in a certain sense the destiny of mankind.... Hence, the importance of discovering the Christian meaning of human suffering.... Putting their generosity into action, young people must never be afraid of suffering viewed in the light of the beatitudes. They must always stay near those who suffer and discover in their own afflictions and those of their brothers the saving value of sorrow, the evangelical strength of all suffering."[15]

In the light of Christ's cross and resurrection, we need to rethink the parameters with which we plan for and search for happiness. We cannot passively copy the models and styles that are handed to us like unopened packages.

True happiness

Human beings are made for happiness. It's the mainspring of human decisions, courage and commitment. A life without the prospect of happiness isn't truly human. Therefore, the question isn't whether a person should seek happiness, but rather how to recognize and to plan for true happiness. The risk of illusion is always present. Today we are unceasingly confronted by various proposals that certainly offer instant gratification but cannot respond to all our expectations. Above all, they are not adequately open to the future.

Augustine passionately searched, experimented and discussed. His tormented journey led him to conclude that the human heart cannot find true peace unless it rests in God: "You made us for yourself, O Lord, and our heart has no peace unless it rests in you."[16] Therefore, he made a bitter and joyous confession: "Late have I loved you, beauty ever ancient and ever new, late have I loved you. You were within me and I was outside, and there I sought you. And evil as I was, I hurled myself on the beautiful things you had created. You were with me and I was not with you. Those creatures kept me far from you, yet if they had not been in you, they would not even have existed. You called, you cried out, you broke through my deafness. You dazzled me, you shone on me and finally cured my blindness."[17]

God gives himself to human beings as utter happiness. He wills that human happiness be his glory. He has placed the need for him within us; the search for happiness is the search for God. Therefore, he is the true explanation of all our desire. We must not limit, shrink or force our desire. We are searchers for the infinite, the eternal, the absolute.

Our culture has taken some important steps in overcoming the spiritualistic reductions of happiness that presuppose a negative or at least suspicious view of the human body. Today we know more clearly that human happiness is found in the whole person.

But we risk new reductions—those centered on pleasure, on possession, on efficiency. Images of this kind of happiness, tied to success, to health, to luxury, are seductive. When they become exclusive, a well-concealed void lies beneath them.

The Gospel permits us to discern when plans for happiness result in illusion, and it strongly calls us back to the whole person: "Though made of body and soul, man is one. Through his bodily composition he gathers to himself the elements of the material world; thus they reach their crown through him, and through him raise their voice in free praise of the creator. For this reason man is not allowed to despise his bodily life; rather, he is obliged to regard his body as good and honorable since God has created it and will raise it up on the last day."[18]

Since true happiness pertains to the whole person, it rejects all whittling down, whatever the reason for it. Neither can it accept being confined to the immediacy of here-and-now experience. This is certainly important, but happiness must carry within itself an opening to the future. The rich man, whose fields had produced abundant harvests, thought he had attained happiness: "'Soul, you have ample goods laid up for many years; take your ease, eat, drink, be merry.' But God said to him, 'Fool! This night your soul is required of you; and the things you have prepared, whose will they be?'" (Lk 12:19-20)

Above all, true happiness means sharing. Happiness acquired because of the suffering of one's brother or sister cannot give us full peace of heart. It's illusory and can't last very long. As soon as possible, those who have been harmed will try to bring the situation to ruin, using all available means, even violence.

We can be happy only if we orient ourselves toward true happiness, following the one route that leads to it: the love that makes us one with others, especially with those who are most in need.

The logic of the cross

The beatitude of those who mourn asks us to enter decisively into the logic of the cross. At first glance this seems harsh, absurd and inhuman. In the paschal mystery of Christ, however, we have become aware that this is the one, real resolution of sin, death and all other forms of evil.

In this regard, the Apostle Paul is particularly decisive: "For Jews demand signs and Greeks seek wisdom, but we preach Christ crucified, a stumbling block to Jews and folly to Gentiles, but to those who are called, both Jews and Greeks, Christ the power of God and the wisdom of God. For the foolishness of God is wiser than men, and the weakness of God is stronger than men" (1 Cor 1:22-25).

John Paul II has dedicated an apostolic letter to this theme: *On the Christian Meaning of Human Suffering (Salvifici Doloris)*. "It assumes different dimensions," he recalls. "Nevertheless, in whatever form, suffering seems to be, and is, almost inseparable from man's earthly existence."[19] The Pope invites us never to think that we can resolve suffering by running away from it. Rather, it must be placed on the cross of Christ—that is, placed within the logic of love. Only in this way can it be defeated; in fact, we experience that "in suffering there is concealed a particular power that draws a person interiorly close to Christ."[20]

Meaningless suffering destroys, but suffering to which we manage to give meaning becomes a wellspring of values and life. Not only does the cross of Christ continue to remind us of this necessity; it also offers the way.

This is an urgent need for our society. Placing suffering within the logic of the cross, and thereby learning love, we can overcome the sense of uselessness, of absurdity, of rebellion that we carry within ourselves. The experience of Paul is renewed: "I complete what is lacking in Christ's afflictions for the sake of his body, that is, the church" (Col 1:24). This is not a theoretical response, but the discovery that we can give meaning: it is the experience that out of sorrow accepted with love we can generate life; it is the sense that nothing goes lost, that everything is inserted into our growth toward salvation.

A quality of life based on ultimates

The beatitudes ask us to enter decisively into the mentality and culture of solidarity. Otherwise, suffering can't take on any meaning. Anyone who has been left alone in failure and sorrow will find it difficult to live constructively. Only a person who feels surrounded and sustained by true solidarity can develop his or her human potential, for the benefit of self and others.

Herein lies one of the greatest challenges for today's believer. Our society prefers to marginalize, to isolate, to ignore those who suffer. If we find ourselves with a dying person, this intensifies the challenge and makes it more absurd. When death can't be experienced as a spectacle, we prefer to keep our distance from the dying, so as not to get involved, but perhaps even more to avoid calling into question the personal equilibrium that we've achieved, basing ourselves more on illusion than on truth.

In the Gospel, instead, the blessed one is the Samaritan who lets himself get involved, changes his course and tries to give a concrete response to the man who has fallen into the hands of robbers (cf. Lk 10:29-37). Only the person who loves effectively is blessed: "By this we know love, that he laid down his life for us; and we ought to lay down our lives for the brethren.... Little children, let us not love in word or speech but in deed and in truth" (1 Jn 3:16, 18).

The beatitudes also ask us to counter another tendency that in certain contexts is particularly strong today: that of basing the quality-of-life concept on the strongest, the healthiest, the most gifted. This clearly has an economic cost, the burden of which all should bear equally. But this is the only way to make our society more human.

A suffering person who is surrounded by true solidarity becomes capable of overcoming the suffering. He or she doesn't let suffering destroy him or her, but rather gives it meaning. One becomes blessed, because together with others, one can help develop those values of presence, of communion, of encounter, of love, that are indispensable to an authentic quality of life for the human community.

For Reflection

John Paul II writes: "The Redeemer suffered in place of man and for man.... In bringing about the Redemption through suffering, Christ has also raised human suffering to the level of the Redemption. Thus each man, in his suffering, can also become a sharer in the redemptive suffering of Christ."[21] This teaching comes down to us from the primitive Church. (Cf., for example, 2 Cor 4:8-11, 14.) What particular influences in our culture today make this teaching hard to remember and/or to practice? What change of perspective do we need?

We talk much about solidarity. But often we stop at the word. The parable of the good Samaritan (cf. Lk 10:29-37) shows that we must change our personal projects, share and place our strength and substance at the disposition of those in need. Do we enter into the dialectic of Jesus, or do we act like the priest and levite—pretending not to see and indifferently continuing on our way, even though people are dying all around us?

Blessed Are the Meek

The harshness that characterizes social relations at all levels today makes it hard for us to open ourselves sincerely to gospel meekness. The atmosphere of violence that we inhale seems to heighten the need for suspicious and defensive attitudes. An intense spirit of competition, swept along by all available means, suggests that it's legitimate to "prevent" the movements of others, so as not to become victims.

Therefore, we must not marvel if the beatitude of meekness sounds like a paradox or an ideal too distant from our possibilities.

One day the father of a family told me: "You're right to propose gospel meekness to young people as an ideal. But you mustn't be surprised if we parents balance matters a little by teaching our children to defend themselves with the same means that others use. Otherwise, we doom them to be crushed by the violence of our society!"

In this context it is more necessary than ever to witness to the value of meekness, and to cultivate the conviction that only this can be the real solution to these problems.

Faithful to the style of Christ

The beatitude about the meek goes right along with that about the poor. In fact, in the Hebrew language the two terms are fused. Gospel meekness is not "an expression of human temperament, but manifests itself where people are in communion with Jesus Christ and become always more conformed to his image through the work of the Spirit."[22]

The Apostle Paul emphasizes meekness as a fruit of the Spirit (cf. Gal 5:23), insofar as it cannot fail to characterize the lives of those who are called to salvation in Christ: "I therefore, a prisoner for the Lord, beg you to lead a life worthy of the calling to which you have been called, with all lowliness and meekness, with patience, forbearing one another in love, eager to maintain the unity of the Spirit in the bond of peace" (Eph 4:1-3).

Evangelical meekness is a gaze that remains fixed on Christ, even when the interior struggle is particularly difficult: "Take my yoke upon you, and learn from me; for I am gentle and lowly in heart, and you will find rest for your souls. For my yoke is easy, and my burden is light" (Mt 11:29-30). Guided by the Spirit, we actualize meekness in our choices and actions. We become a living memory, a transparent sign, a humble and courageous announcement of the meekness of the Redeemer.

Throughout his life Jesus was the meek and courageous servant of truth, who placed all his trust in the mission he received from the Father and in his innate power to make himself recognized and accepted as such a servant. In this sense, the clear-cut *"no"* to the temptations in the desert is significant (cf. Mt 4:1-10; Mk 1:12-13; Lk 4:1-13). Being definitive, the truth entrusted to Jesus cannot be accepted in a wave of enthusiasm over instant gratification of concrete needs or because of the showiness of miraculous deeds or the fascination exercised by power. This truth must be proposed in such a way as to be recognized and chosen by everyone as what he or she has always sought.

Thus, putting aside the very glory of his "equality with God" (cf. Phil 2:5-11), Jesus totally dedicated himself to "preach good news to the poor. He has sent me to proclaim release to the captives and recovering of sight to the blind, to set at liberty those who are oppressed, to proclaim the acceptable year of the Lord" (Lk 4:18-19). This was to be done without violence, exploitation or imposition: "He will not wrangle or cry aloud, nor will any one hear his voice in the streets; he will not break a bruised reed or quench a smoldering wick, till he brings justice to victory; and in his name will the Gentiles hope" (Mt 12:19-21).

Christ's meekness carried him to the cross, which he transformed into resurrection. Thus, he can ask his disciples to take it up also, as the only wisdom and only energy that can truly determine history (cf. 1 Cor 1:17-25). He requires that meekness determine all their choices: "You have heard that it was said, 'An eye for an eye and a tooth for a tooth.' But I say to you, Do not resist one who is evil. But if any one strikes you on the right cheek, turn to him the other also" (Mt 5:38-39). They must not close their hearts even to those who do evil to them: "You have heard that it was said, 'You shall love your neighbor and hate your enemy.' But I say to you, Love your enemies and pray for those who persecute you, so that you may be sons of your Father who is in heaven; for he makes his sun rise on the evil and on the good, and sends rain on the just and on the unjust" (Mt 5:43-45).

Nonviolence

Nonviolence is one of those issues about which people have strong feelings. It is proposed, discussed and studied at all levels. When the tension at the social or international levels becomes stronger, the debate takes on tones that are particularly sharp, even marked by ideological overtones.

In this context, the witness of Christian meekness acquires new urgency, despite accusations that come from some quarters in the name of efficiency and the need for action. And the young are called to be in the vanguard.

First of all, a clearer awareness must be fostered regarding the depth and breadth of the violence that permeates society. In the face of particularly shocking episodes, it isn't hard to react. But unless we seek to identify and remove the roots of violence, our reaction is sterile. It's enough to reflect on the language and actions of daily life to recognize at once how deep and widespread violence is.

A journey of true conversion is indispensable. Repression and domination—even if sometimes necessary—never truly resolve problems. The conscience must be reached, to create a new mentality and promote a culture based on nonviolence. We must announce the necessity that each one's heart become the heart of a neighbor toward others, beginning with those who are most in need (cf. Lk 10:29-37).

Persons who are meek according to the Gospel base sincere respect for others on an active commitment to solidarity. They never consider it lawful to manipulate or constrain a neighbor's liberty, for they recall that the dignity of the "image" and the "child" of God always resides in every person, even when disguised, neglected and trampled upon. Rather, the more this dignity is denied, the more the meek feel called to place themselves in solidarity with the downtrodden to reaffirm and develop it.

To this end, the meek person begins with a trusting attitude. This doesn't mean naiveté. It is certitude that only in this way can we open others to the values of justice, fraternity and peace. This is the face of God that Christ reveals to us: "In this the love of God was made manifest among us, that God sent his only Son into the world, so that we might live through him.... We love, because he first loved us" (1 Jn 4:9, 19).

We well know that nonviolent solutions demand more commitment, more energy, more time. In fact, we are often blamed for placing impediments or retarding resolutions of problems. But this must not discourage us. We are certain that this is the one way to give a fully human and lasting response.

There is another risk that it would be naive to undervalue: meekness could transform itself into unintentional connivance with the violent or be exploited by others from this perspective. We must be vigilant. Meekness should never signify lack of commitment toward those who undergo violence. Instead, we must loyally take their part, personally risking, personally paying.

When we want to bring meekness into the social-political sphere, it isn't always easy to identify the most constructive steps. Situations are complex. This makes it more urgent to be committed to the correct formation of conscience and the acquisition of sufficient competence.

Conscience and reciprocity

Cultivation of and respect for conscience constitute the other dimension of gospel meekness that we are called to emphasize today. The appeal of John Paul II for the world day of peace in 1991 is significant: "The person can not be treated as a kind of object, governed exclusively by forces outside his control. To the contrary, notwithstanding his fragility, he is not deprived of the capacity to search for and freely know the good, to recognize and reject evil, to choose the truth and oppose error." In this respect, faith provides even more definite horizons and foundations: "God, creating the human person, has inscribed in his heart a law that everyone can find (cf. Rom 2:15), and the conscience is itself the capacity to discern and to act according to this law: to obey it is the proper dignity of man."

The dignity proper to each human person requires that everyone have a profound respect for individual conscience. Clearly, this does not mean lack of interest in the truth; rather, the sincere search for truth is essential to the very dignity of the person. However, truth is to be sought for according to the dictates of conscience. "All men," affirms Vatican II, "are bound to seek the truth, especially in what concerns God and his Church, and to embrace the truth they come to know and hold fast to it." The Council adds that these obligations bind man's conscience, because "truth cannot impose itself except by virtue of its own truth, as it makes its entrance into the mind at once quietly and with power."[23]

In fidelity to Christ, Christian meekness witnesses to this intrinsic strength of truth. At the same time it witnesses to trust in human beings and in their desire for the true, despite all difficulties and egoisms.

The context in which we live has a great need for this witness. Too often, in fact, the manner of handling information is violent and induces to violence. The right to information is certainly fundamental, but it cannot be exercised by crushing the weakest. Christian meekness must become a courageous search for a way of communicating that effectively permits receivers to arrive at truth and to adhere to it because it is such.

The meek according to the Gospel do everything they can to journey together toward the truth, each one profiting from the progress and contributions of the others. To proclaim Christ is always to know him better. Even from those who are more distant from Christianity, the believer derives something that clarifies and further illumines the face of Christ.

Respect for conscience will spur us to promote the

true participation of everyone in decision-making processes at all levels. Christian meekness is a decisive "no" to any form whatsoever of undue pressure and conditioning. It loyally commits itself to the real participation of all, convinced that only by a common search, in respect and reciprocal listening, is it possible to identify the best solutions and put them into effect.

The witness of gospel meekness is more urgent where intimidation is bolder and more violent. It then takes on a courageous and active solidarity that permits even the more vulnerable to refuse to be blackmailed or to submit to any other form of violent intimidation.

The same decisiveness should also be used in rejecting other forms of violence, to which unfortunately we may not always pay enough attention, since they are more subtle and hidden.

Above all, however, gospel meekness must permit the Christian community to live its interior diversity as reciprocal enrichment. Then Christians will be able to be faithful to that unity, the fruit of love, which Christ has bound up with the credibility of the proclamation of the Gospel (cf. Jn 17:20-21).

For Reflection

In our times we are better able to understand the factors at the root of human violence. But often our analysis stops at the threshold of the responsibility—especially if it's our own—or else we want to find a scapegoat. Doesn't it seem to you that by acting this way we reinforce the phenomenon of violence? Can you pinpoint a need for real conversion that begins with yourself?

Meekness is often presented as naiveté, idealism or inefficiency. Christ reminded the twelve: "Behold, I send you out as sheep in the midst of wolves; so be wise as serpents and innocent as doves" (Mt 10:16). How can we reconcile these two examples of Jesus to clarify the meaning of Christian meekness?

There are many non-violent movements in our society. Certainly all of them have positive points, yet there is also some obscurity about each. In the light of gospel meekness, try to read about those that are active in your locality. Does any of them have a truly Christian orientation toward which you can direct yourself and your desires for peace and non-violence?

Blessed Are Those Who Hunger and Thirst for Justice

"Do not lay up for yourselves treasures on earth, where moth and rust consume and where thieves break in and steal, but lay up for yourselves treasure in heaven, where neither moth nor rust consumes and where thieves do not break in and steal. For where your treasure is, there will your heart be also" (Mt 6:19-21).

The treasure that is not consumed and that must focus our heart is the justice that God gives us in Christ. It signifies communion, life, fullness and happiness. We need to opt radically for it, as does the person who finds a treasure in a field and covers it up: "then in his joy he goes and sells all that he has and buys that field;" or like the merchant that "on finding one pearl of great value, went and sold all that he had and bought it" (Mt 13:44-46).

We must be watchful so that the justice that the Father gives us in Christ may always remain our life's priority, the focus of our desires. We cannot offer a thousand justifications, as did the people invited to the great banquet: "I have bought a field, and I must go out and see it.... I have bought five yoke of oxen, and I go to examine them.... I have married a wife...." For these, the owner of the house has strong words: "For I tell you, none of those men who were invited shall taste my banquet" (Lk 14:18-24).

Every desire and preoccupation must let itself be confirmed by what is definitive: "But seek first his kingdom and his righteousness, and all these things shall be yours as well" (Mt 6:33).

All this must not encourage us to escape from concrete commitments on the social and economic levels.

The justice that God gives us is not an alternative or a lack of responsibility in this regard. However, this justice does ask to be the foundation and horizon of all other projects of justice.

The final message of the Synod on the Laity of 1987 is significant: "The Holy Spirit helps us see more clearly that today holiness is not possible without commitment to justice, without solidarity with the poor and the oppressed."[24] Vatican II, after affirming that Christian hope "does not diminish the importance of intervening duties but rather undergirds the acquittal of them with fresh incentives," continues: "By contrast, when a divine substructure and the hope of eternal life are wanting, man's dignity is most grievously lacerated, as current events often attest; riddles of life and death, of guilt and of grief, go unsolved, with the frequent result that men succumb to despair."[25]

To hunger and thirst for justice means to remain totally open toward the gift of God and totally committed to the challenges of history. "With these words," recalls John Paul II, "Jesus invites us to holiness, to justice and to perfection, which arise from a listening to the word of God which has been made a lifestyle, social conduct and daily existence.... The authentic Christian must responsibly take on the burden of the social needs that arise from his faith. The vision of the world and of life that the Gospel gives and that Catholic social doctrine explains impels us to constructive action much more than some ideology, no matter how attractive it may appear."[26]

A justice born of love

The justice that the Father gives us in Christ is the fruit of love. It makes us all children in the only Son. We

must therefore live as brothers and sisters. We are all equal in our dignity as children, but we have relationships of complementarity toward one another, because of the various gifts that each has been given for the good of all. The Apostle Paul emphasizes this constantly: "For in Christ Jesus you are all sons of God, through faith. For as many of you as were baptized into Christ have put on Christ. There is neither Jew nor Greek, there is neither slave nor free, there is neither male nor female; for you are all one in Christ Jesus" (Gal 3:26-28).

Discrimination has no more reason to exist; privileges can no longer be legitimate; to overpower others must be seen as sin.

The more our heart opens itself to the experience of the justice given to us in Christ, the more it will feel the urgency of seeing this affirmed at all levels. But it is necessary to act in such a way that even when we fearlessly denounce those who cause injustice, the justice that we build up in society may be a responsibility of true love: "Weep and howl for the miseries that are coming upon you.... Behold, the wages of the laborers who mowed your fields, which you kept back by fraud, cry out; and the cries of the harvesters have reached the ears of the Lord of hosts" (Jas 5:1, 4).

The beatitudes permit us to unmask the many reductive forms of justice with which we often silence our conscience.

Those just persons whom the Gospel declares blessed are constantly searching to see whether what is declared to be just is actually so in fact. They are sincerely committed to creating conditions that permit all to enjoy their rights; they always question any form of privilege, bringing to light any injustice that lies behind it.

In a word: justice according to the Gospel always gives itself as a pledge of loyal participation in the processes that permit justice to become real. But this participation is not dictated by hate or by a desire for revenge, but by a love that does not recognize limits in its preoccupations and horizons.

Solidarity with all who seek justice

Therefore, the Christian community feels a profound solidarity with everyone who struggles for justice. The Church well knows that it doesn't have ready-made prescriptions for healing the grave ills that history continues to bring before us; but it knows equally well that it can bring a contribution, a stimulus and a perspective to the search for and implementation of appropriate solutions.

Reflecting on the dramatic situation of many underdeveloped peoples, John Paul II writes: "The Church does not have technical solutions to offer.... Nor does she show preference for one or the other, provided that human dignity is properly respected and promoted, and provided she herself is allowed the room she needs to exercise her ministry in the world. But the Church is an 'expert in humanity,' and this leads her necessarily to extend her religious mission to the various fields in which man and women expend their efforts in search of the always relative happiness which is possible in this world, in line with their dignity as persons."[27]

The instrument with which the Christian community brings this contribution is its social doctrine. This is not an ideology, but rather "the accurate formulation of the results of a careful reflection on the complex realities of human existence, in society and in the international order, in the light of faith and of the Church's tradition." This doctrine, therefore, proposes to "interpret" social realities, "determining their conformity with or divergence from the lines of the Gospel teaching on man and his vocation, a vocation which is at once earthly and transcendent," and orienting, therefore, Christian behavior.[28]

This calls for mature consciences that can courageously denounce evil in all its forms, but above all that can creatively point out possibilities and hopes: in the last analysis that can announce Christ and his new and definitive justice.

The consciences needed should be, as Vatican II emphasized, capable of blending professional competence and clear ethical perspectives, a sense of values and a capacity for discerning possibilities in history, coherence with the truth known in Christ and cooperation with those that pursue the same objectives, a sense of one's own responsibility and respectful attention to the indications given by the magisterium of the Church.[29]

For the development of such consciences, a deeper study and assimilation of the Church's social teachings is particularly urgent.

Political commitment

Hunger and thirst for justice must lead us to develop a mentality sincerely convinced of the centrality and concreteness of the common good. The new forms of individualism that characterize today's lifestyle make this commitment more difficult and at the same time more urgent. It's necessary to begin from the earliest stage of formation, yet if we want to be coherent in our everyday choices, we must continue to deepen this mentality.

The common good "embraces the sum of those conditions of the social life whereby men, families and associations more adequately and readily may attain their own perfection."[30]

In order to delineate correctly the content of the common good and thus make it a reality, the active and responsible participation of everyone is necessary. Indispensable are the confrontation, dialogue and mediation that only a correct political dynamic can guarantee. Desire for justice must lead the Christian community to render its own participation always more convinced and generous, not so as to secure power or privilege, but to affirm justice ever more clearly in fraternity and peace.

In our attitude toward politics, we often let ourselves be influenced by bitter experiences, suspicions more or less justifiable and examples that give little encouragement. Some hold it impossible to remain true to one's conscience, so they withdraw from any participation.

John Paul II has written: "In order to achieve their task directed to the Christian animation of the temporal order, in the sense of serving persons and society, the lay faithful are never to relinquish their participation in 'public life,' that is, in the many different economic, social, legislative, administrative and cultural areas which are intended to promote organically and institutionally the common good."[31]

The ways to concretize political commitment must be decided in the light of the vocation, talents and life choices of each individual: "Every person," John Paul II also recalls, "has a right and duty to participate in public life, albeit in a diversity and complementarity of forms, levels, tasks and responsibilities."[32] Neither can it be omitted that "the Church praises and esteems the work of those who for the good of men devote themselves to the service of the state and take on the burdens of this office."[33]

Whatever its form, the believer's political commitment must be characterized by a true spirit of service, dictated by love and justice. We are all convinced of this in words, but in deeds—both small and great—we often behave differently. It's enough to reflect on the promptness with which we transform our own position in the workplace into "power."

Equally important is our living relationship with the community to which we belong. In fact, as Paul VI emphasized, the Christian community is "to discern the options and commitments which are called for in order to bring about the social, political and economic changes seen in many cases to be urgently needed."[34] In such a context the inevitable differences of opinion will not develop into polarization, but into mutual enrichment that brings everyone closer to the truth, as Vatican II reminds us: "They should always try to enlighten one another through honest discussion, preserving mutual charity and caring above all for the common good."[35]

For Reflection

"Coherence of life is of the utmost importance for the lay faithful," affirms the Synod of 1987. "They have to become holy in their ordinary professional and social life. So that they can correspond to their vocation, the lay faithful must regard the activities of daily life as opportunities to be united with God and to accomplish his will and also to serve other human beings, bringing them to communion with God in Christ."[36] Are you able to plan your everyday commitments according to this perspective?

We are always prompt to claim our rights. But we are slower to recognize that these also give us duties: to do responsibly what is within our competence for their realization; to recognize that others have the same rights; to reach harmony with them. If we forget the duties, don't we depreciate the rights themselves, preventing them from delineating the whole of social life?

Catholic social doctrine is a fundamental wealth for the entire faith community and each of the baptized. Are you sufficiently aware of this doctrine? What has been your interest, for example, regarding the most recent encyclicals? Have you read them?

Blessed Are the Merciful

There is no book in the Bible that does not indicate mercy as the fundamental feature of God's face: "The Lord your God is a merciful God; he will not fail you or destroy you or forget the covenant with your fathers which he swore to them" (Dt 4:31). The psalmist never tires of singing: "Praise the Lord! O give thanks to the Lord, for he is good; for his steadfast love endures for ever!" (Ps 106:1); "O Israel, hope in the Lord! For with the Lord there is steadfast love, and with him is plenteous redemption" (Ps 130:7). And Isaiah has recourse to touching images: "Can a woman forget her sucking child, that she should have no compassion on the son of her womb? Even these may forget, yet I will not forget you. Behold, I have graven you on the palms of my hands" (Is 49:15-16).

At the threshold of the New Testament, Mary proclaims: "His mercy is on those who fear him from generation to generation" (Lk 1:50). Then Christ, with his paschal mystery of death and resurrection, shows without further shadow of doubt the fathomless depths of the Father's mercy. John Paul II writes: "In Christ and through Christ, God also becomes especially visible in his mercy." In fact, "Not only does he speak of it and explain it by the use of comparisons and parables, but above all he himself makes it incarnate and personifies it. He himself, in a certain sense, is mercy. To the person who sees it in him—and finds it in him—God becomes 'visible' in a particular way as the Father 'who is rich in mercy'" (Eph 2:4).[37]

Someone who exercises mercy according to the Gospel is blessed because he or she has strongly experienced God and has felt transformed by him. The merciful person has encountered the merciful face of God,

Christ, and has been captured by it. One sees oneself pardoned, renewed and enlivened, not by personal merits or works, but solely by love.

This leads to a sincere decision to imprint all relations with one's brothers and sisters with that same mercy. One knows that in giving mercy, one will receive it, but also that the greater the mercy received, the greater the mercy to be given in turn.

John Paul II reminded young adults: "Mercy, as Jesus taught and practiced it, 'rich in mercy,' is the most authentic aspect of love.... Merciful love is not simply compassion when confronted with those who suffer.... It is not passivity, but decisive action, born of faith, on behalf of the neighbor.... The witness of service and of fraternity given by today's youth is one of the most stupendous things in our world—something that gives great consolation."[38]

Gratitude for the gift

Throughout the history of the Christian community we find remarkable pages about its courage in being faithful to the witness and proclamation of mercy.

But sometimes concern not to trivialize God's transcendence and also the consistency of life required by faith make the Christian community less strong in witnessing to God's mercy. At the sacramental level there have been procedures that discouraged people from approaching Communion frequently; at the moral level, rigorous impositions; at the level of announcement, an underlying fear. Even today it is possible to notice elements of this scant attention to God's mercy, accompanied by emphasis on his majesty and justice.

In reality, as John Paul II writes: "Love, so to speak, conditions justice and, in the final analysis, justice serves love. The primacy and superiority of love vis-à-vis justice...are revealed precisely through mercy. This seemed so obvious to the psalmists and prophets that the very term justice ended up by meaning the salvation accomplished by the Lord and his mercy."[39]

Mercy acts in such wise that God never tires to take the initiative in regard to human beings. He does not let himself be blocked by refusal, but proposes, calls and gives himself incessantly. He remains always turned toward us as one who eases our yoke or stoops down to feed us (cf. Hos 11:4). He tosses all our sins behind him and sweeps them away like mist (cf. Is 38:17, 44:22).

The certainty that God's love and mercy came first is fundamental to the whole Christian life: "In this the love of God was made manifest among us, that God sent his only Son into the world, so that we might live through him. In this is love, not that we loved God but that he loved us and sent his Son" (1 Jn 4:9-10).

In the moment of farewell, Christ reminds the disciples: "Greater love has no man than this, that a man lay down his life for his friends. You are my friends if you do what I command you. No longer do I call you servants, for the servant does not know what his master is doing; but I have called you friends, for all that I have heard from my Father I have made known to you" (Jn 15:13-15).

The relationship that God offers to human beings is one of love, of life, of fullness and not of imposition or negation. Christ "emptied Himself" of the divine glory in order to make us certain that he comes to give us his fullness (cf. Phil 2:5-11). Gazing upon the cross, then, who can think that his or her life does not rest on the loving mercy of the Father? "If God is for us, who is against us? He who did not spare his own Son but gave him up for us all, will he not also give us all things with him? Who shall bring any charge against God's elect? It is God who justifies; who is to condemn? Is it Christ Jesus, who died, yes, who was raised from the dead, who is at the right hand of God, who indeed intercedes for us?" (Rom 8:31-34)

A sign for our brothers and sisters

The experience of God's mercy imprints on the Christian life an image of profound generosity, freeing it from slavery to fear and opening it to trust at every level. The Apostle Paul decisively reminded the Roman Christians of this: "For you did not receive the spirit of slavery to fall back into fear, but you have received the spirit of sonship. When we cry, 'Abba! Father!' it is the Spirit himself bearing witness with our spirit that we are children of God" (Rom 8:15-16). And he added that this filial security must make us stronger in the face of any difficulty whatsoever: in all these things "we are more than conquerors through him who loved us," because nothing "will be able to separate us from the love of God in Christ Jesus our Lord" (Rom 8:37, 39).

Those who exercise gospel mercy don't let themselves be discouraged by the limitations and failures that they experience on their journey. They don't withdraw from the sources of grace; rather, they approach them with greater resolve and confidence. St. Alphonsus de Liguori opposed the pastoral tendency of his times, the eighteenth century, which emphasized human unworthiness and made it difficult to approach the sacraments, especially the Eucharist. "This venom does not recognize itself," he wrote, "and one dies before sensing that one has been poisoned.... I know that the angels are not worthy of it, but Jesus Christ has made man worthy of it to raise him up in his miseries. From this sacrament we have every good: without this help, everything collapses."[40]

Conduct toward our neighbor must be coherent with the mercy we have received. To act otherwise would be senseless. The condemnation of the unmerciful servant who had been forgiven by his master but would not do the same for his companion who owed him only a small sum is especially strong: "You wicked servant! I forgave you all that debt because you besought me; and should not you have had mercy on your fellow servant, as I had mercy on you?" (Mt 18:32-33).

Consistency between the mercy received and the mercy given to one's brothers and sisters is so important that Christ asked his disciples to make it the object of a special request to the Father: "Forgive us our debts, as we also have forgiven our debtors" (Mt 6:12). Peter, who already felt that forgiving seven times was generous, received the reply: "I do not say to you seven times, but seventy times seven" (Mt 18:22). Nor are we to draw the line after giving pardon to those who ask it, we must be ready to take the initiative toward reconciliation: "So if you are offering your gift at the altar, and there remember that your brother has something against you, leave your gift there before the altar and go; first be reconciled to your brother, and then come and offer your gift" (Mt 5:23-24).

Therefore, the boundary of all moral growth can be none other than mercy, as Luke writes: "Be merciful, even as your Father is merciful" (Lk 6:36).

Sharing and not judging

"By becoming for people a model of merciful love for others, Christ proclaims by his actions even more than by his words that call to mercy which is one of the essential elements of the Gospel ethos. In this instance it is not just a case of fulfilling a commandment or an obligation of an ethical nature; it is also a case of satisfying a condition of major importance for God to reveal himself in his mercy to man."[41]

It is certainly not easy to consistently live by these perspectives. Often they seem too distant from our contemporary social context. Not a few people hold that to open oneself in mercy is to become too vulnerable or to make the solutions to various problems still more difficult.

In reality, gospel mercy does not ask that justice and its demands be set aside. Rather, mercy urges us to make justice more human and more incisive, to open it to love, without which it is difficult to identify and to bring about solutions worthy of human beings.

The role that volunteerism is assuming in our society eloquently confirms this. Volunteerism is not opposed to the far-reaching response that must come from official structures; much less can these latter shirk their own responsibilities. Rather, both types of activity are to be integrated, to allow new needs to be addressed more directly and to give better quality to the responses.

It's necessary to develop a coherent interdependence between justice and love. This interdependence is indispensable for both. Without love, justice would lose touch with the concrete needs of individuals; without justice, love would not be able to untie the structural knots which cause so much suffering.

Structures, relationships and negotiations are for persons. To so objectify and bureaucratize them that this vision is lost is to empty them not only of meaning but also of effectiveness. Mercy tends to so act that in all structures the centrality of the person is always clear, so that general statements of rights flow into concrete responses to the real needs of all, beginning with those of the more weak and defenseless.

Concretely, mercy asks that a sincere attitude of acceptance be developed, quick to tune into the needs of others.

It is indispensable, then, to free ourselves not only from all prejudices, old and new, but also from the habit of immediately imprisoning others in judgments that admit of no appeal. The words of Christ in this regard are clear: "Judge not, and you will not be judged; condemn not, and you will not be condemned" (Lk 6:37). And the Apostle Paul, after referring to mutual respect for conscience, exhorts: "Then let us no more pass judgment on one another, but rather decide never to put a stumbling block or hindrance in the way of a brother" (Rom 14:13).

It's necessary to listen, to understand and to share, if we want to become a message of hope for our brothers and sisters. Then it will be possible to journey together and, each acting responsibly, to overcome the power of evil in all its forms. Only thus will we become convincing signs of the presence of Christ, who came among us not to judge the world but to save it (cf. Jn 12:47).

For Reflection

In the heart of the Easter Vigil the Church proclaims: "How boundless your merciful love! To ransom a slave you gave away your Son. O happy fault, O necessary sin of Adam, which gained for us so great a Redeemer!" Is this the perspective within which you view your shortcomings and faults? Do you feel that the sacrament of Reconciliation is a sacrament of joy?

In our society we often disguise our lack of interest in another's choices as respect for him or her. Gospel mercy impels us to be firm instead, so that all may open themselves to the truth. What steps can be taken so that proposals and respect won't be in opposition, even if it isn't always easy to find a way to validly combine them?

Are you a volunteer? In what area? Does the complexity of local, national and global needs tug at your heart?

Blessed Are the Pure of Heart

There has been and continues to be much discussion about this beatitude. Interpretations show the influence not only of the meaning that various cultures assign to the body, but also of the way in which the relationship between faith and works is perceived. Already in the first Christian community there were differences: "Paul and John have come nearer than others to its universal and liberating scope, while in later and current writings there is a tendency to be ethically limited. The history of this concept shows how the witnesses of the New Testament fought for an evangelical concept of purity, and how great is the danger of relapsing into a legalistic mentality regarding purity."[42]

What is at issue here is a fundamental requirement which faith cannot renounce. It's clear that belief always tends to become life. To be responsibly inserted in the history of salvation calls for consistent choices in tune with this history. Otherwise, persons fall into dangerous illusions, which have been forcefully denounced in the Gospel (cf. Mt 7:21). But faith must proclaim with equal clarity that salvation is a free gift; it is justification wrought by the infinite love of God; it is new life that springs from baptismal rebirth. Good behavior is fruit of this grace: it expresses it and makes it develop toward fullness.

Evangelical purity, therefore, concerns the whole person. It is not restricted to the areas of affectivity or sexuality. These dimensions are certainly part of it; in fact, today, in the context of the erotic consumerism that surrounds us, they are to be witnessed to more courageously. But we must never lose the reference to the totality of the person, unified by a purified heart and renewed by the Spirit. Any reduction whatsoever is to be avoided, beginning with signs of mistrust or suspicion with regard to the body and sexuality, which would make it still more difficult to understand evangelical purity.

The heart and its intentions

The marked pluralism that characterizes our society tells us that personalities must be mature, consistent and capable of making discernments. Before preoccupying ourselves over individual attitudes or actions we must take care to graft ourselves profoundly onto Christ and remain in his love (cf. Jn 15:1-11).

Purity lies not so much in what a person does as in his or her inner life, intentions and conscience: "Do you not see that whatever goes into the mouth passes into the stomach, and so passes on? But what comes out of the mouth proceeds from the heart, and this defiles a man. For out of the heart come evil thoughts, murder, adultery, fornication, theft, false witness, slander. These are what defile a man" (Mt 15:17-20).

Good fruits can come only from a pure heart. A heart that is not pure distorts even what is basically good. The life of the believer is thus characterized by a circular dynamic that goes from heart to actions and back to heart. The heart is the root that gives ultimate value. Actions are fruits that reveal and reinforce the "quality" of the heart: "Either make the tree good, and its fruit good; or make the tree bad, and its fruit bad; for the tree is known by its fruit.... The good man out of his good treasure brings forth good, and the evil man out of his evil treasure brings forth evil" (Mt 12:33-35).

All this means entering into the logic of the new justice, superior to that of the scribes and pharisees (cf. Mt 5:17-20). This is possible thanks to the new dynamic of life and freedom that the Spirit establishes within us (cf.

Rom 8:2), realizing the prophetic promise: "A new heart I will give you, and a new spirit I will put within you; and I will take out of your flesh the heart of stone and give you a heart of flesh. And I will put my spirit within you, and cause you to walk in my statutes and be careful to observe my ordinances" (Ez 36:26-27).

Today we better understand the role of intention in the whole moral life, and we recognize it as the element that, in the last analysis, determines the value of what we do. The development of psychology and the other human sciences has improved our knowledge of the dynamic of the moral decision.

But intention has to be seen in all its dimensions. It has to express the tension toward the fullness that is proper to our nature, by virtue of our creation and our filial adoption in Christ. It must declare the meaning of our life, of our vocation.

It's understandable why spiritual tradition insists so much on purity of intention. St. Alphonsus says: "The intention, good or evil, with which we do something, makes it good or evil in God's eyes.... Purity of intention is called heavenly alchemy, through which iron becomes gold. It should be said that the most trivial and ordinary actions, done to please God, become acts of divine love."[43]

Gospel purity increases the unity and depth of all our activity, illuminating it with the meaning and plan of life that we have singled out and chosen. Even if the difficulties are great, the pure heart's decisions spring from its life orientation. It well knows that, by the power of the Spirit received in Baptism, one can free oneself from every slavery and debt, make personal decisions, choose according to conscience.

Pure intention also assures greater clarity and strength for the life project, opening it to always more vast horizons. The fidelity of the pure heart does not consist in an almost mechanical repetition of actions or of attitudes, but in passing from newness to newness "until we all attain to the unity of the faith and of the knowledge of the Son of God, to mature manhood, to the measure of the stature of the fullness of Christ" (Eph 4:13).

Thus, purity of intention spurs us on to ever deepen our loving union with the will of God. Christ proclaims of himself: "I can do nothing on my own authority...but [I do] the will of him who sent me" (Jn 5:30). He adds that his food is "to do the will" of the Father and "to accomplish his work" (Jn 4:34). Even in the face of the impending cross, in the Garden of Olives, he prays: "My Father, if it be possible, let this cup pass from me; nevertheless, not as I will, but as thou wilt" (Mt 26:39). He asks, therefore, that the disciples make the Father's will the object of confident prayer: "Our Father...thy kingdom come, thy will be done, on earth as it is in heaven" (Mt 6:9-10). To its loving accomplishment is linked entrance into the reign of heaven (cf. Mt 7:21), since "whoever does the will of my Father in heaven is my brother, and sister, and mother" (Mt 12:50).

However, one must live of love that has decided to become one sole thing with the plan of God, certain that in this lies the secret of fullness and of happiness. Today this dimension needs to be emphasized with major attention, in faithfulness to the word of Christ: "If you keep my commandments, you will abide in my love, just as I have kept my Father's commandments and abide in his love. These things I have spoken to you, that my joy may be in you, and that your joy may be full" (Jn 15:10-11).

The challenge of needs

Purity of heart identifies itself always more closely with love, the "new commandment" that summarizes the whole of the Christian moral imperative (cf. Jn 15:1-17), the great charism that permits all others to be lived authentically, that is, as gifts for the good of all (cf. 1 Cor 13). St. Augustine appeals to a charming example: "Because of its weight, every body tends toward the place that is appropriate for it. Fire tends toward the heights, rock toward the depths, both of them impelled by their weight to seek their own places. Oil poured into water rises to the top, water poured into oil immerses itself beneath the oil, both of them pushed by their weight to seek their proper places.... My own weight is love; it takes me everywhere I take myself."[44]

The Church asks us to consider this obligation of Christian love. "God's generosity does not measure itself according to human needs—it is infinitely greater than these. In their turn, therefore, the Church and each Christian must permeate all forms of service to humankind with generosity and liberality. This includes forms of service that are more remote from professional, social or political commitment; all are to be characterized by universal openness, preference for persons and readiness for self-sacrifice. At the same time Christians must always be aware that no personal commitment can adequately manifest the love of God, which surpasses every expectation and desire."[45]

This is the tension that we see shining through the whole life of Paul: "For the love of Christ controls us, because we are convinced that one has died for all; therefore all have died. And he died for all, that those who live might live no longer for themselves but for him who for their sake died and was raised" (2 Cor 5:14-15).

Our very memory should grow in purity, communicating the grateful memory of the love of Christ in the paschal mystery. The more we cultivate this grateful memory, the more will love become our true intention: the more pure will we be.

All this requires profound uprightness of conscience. We must discern our real motivations by clarifying and examining them. And this is also true regarding our needs, which today have become the object of manipulations that reach always farther and deeper. This doesn't mean denying what we are actually living. In the long run, we would fall into a voluntarism that couldn't last. Rather, we need to discover up to what point our experiences are the result of pressures from games that are being played at our expense. Having carried out this discernment, we will be able to integrate our needs into the whole of our reality and respond to them not only out of our experience, but also on the basis of the dignity and totality of the person.

Being transparent

This intention to transmit God's love makes us feel and act as "neighbor" to every person, without discrimination or restricted horizons. The parable of the good Samaritan makes it clear that instead of asking who our neighbor is, we must sincerely check to see whether we make ourselves neighbors (cf. Lk 10:29-37).

A pure heart results in a pure glance. It doesn't reduce another person to body that is an object of desire (cf. Mt 5:27-28) but always sees in him or her the dignity of "image" and "child"—which nothing can completely destroy. In fact, when the ups and downs of life lead another person to forget or try to deny this image, one who is pure of heart wants to manifest and foster it. With respect and honesty, the Christian who is pure of heart testifies that this divine image can be reaffirmed; with joy and simplicity he or she offers all the help possible.

A pure heart is not timidly closed in on itself. Instead, it is open toward others, things and the whole of reality. In the various events that take place, it perceives the presence of God, who brings salvation history to completion: it makes us see God. But it does not let us limit ourselves only to contemplating him; it impels us to accept and promptly respond to the gift and appeal addressed to us.

Our whole person then becomes a "transparency" of the God who is transforming us and all of reality. Purity of heart certainly sets our affectivity in motion, but not only this. Embodied as we are, we are called to become convincing transparencies of the love of Christ. The visibility of charity "must be accompanied by a sort of transparency, which does not fix attention on itself, but invites a prolonged look at God."[46]

The gist of these perspectives must be an affective maturity that grows always less cloudy. We need to react against erotic consumerism, which is becoming a widespread form of alienation.[47] However, all this must not mean withdrawal from others or fear of them, much less scorn for the body and sexuality. It implies, rather, transparent presence, communion, the gift of person to person. Purity of heart is, in fact, profound liberty which transforms itself into real charity, mindful that "love is of God, and he who loves is born of God and knows God. He who does not love does not know God; for God is love" (1 Jn 4:7-8).

It is important, recalls John Paul II, "to educate young people to 'beautiful love' in order to distance them from all the assaults that are bent on destroying the treasure of their youth—drugs, violence and sin in general—and to orient them toward the way that leads to God: in Christian marriage, the actual road toward human realization and sanctification for the majority of men and women; and also, when Christ calls, in the radical giving required by the priestly or religious vocation. Today the Church needs many apostles to evangelize the world of the new millennium which is approaching."[49]

For Reflection

Results are what count most in our society. These are what determine the goodness or the evil, the value or the uselessness, the correctness or the incorrectness of our actions. Looking at results, we are sometimes disposed to legitimize absurd behaviors or to denounce any further questioning as useless. Try to discuss some experience that shows how all this ends by draining our actions of true meaning.

The guidelines that the Christian community offers in regard to sexual ethics are often contested because they are understood as restricting liberty and spontaneity. But, instead, these guidelines are meant to guarantee personal dignity and authenticity to our behavior in the area of sexuality. Is this viewpoint difficult for you to appreciate? What are the greater difficulties? How do you respond to them?

The development of a life orientation is a fundamental aspect of young adulthood. Today, the objective difficulties of doing what we personally want to do sharpen the fear of long-term binding decisions. In all this, the vocational perspective calls for greater trust. How does this correspond to your self-orientation for life?

Blessed Are the Peacemakers

Peace is the value that we are most clearly conscious of today. We are always more convinced that without peace everything will collapse and the very survival of humanity and of our planet will be called into question. Moreover, we recognize that the quality of life, to which we are particularly sensitive, is possible only if the investments and structures of war are reconverted and placed at the service of peace.

Vatican II affirms: "Moving gradually together and everywhere more conscious already of its unity, [the human] family cannot accomplish its task of constructing for all men everywhere a world more genuinely human unless each person devotes himself to the cause of peace with renewed vigor."[49]

There is also a growing awareness that peace requires the participation of all. It is everyone's responsibility and cannot be delegated sight unseen to the powerful or elite of society. Pacifist movements and initiatives are becoming ever more numerous.

This is certainly a sign of the times, and one of the most positive. Participation is expected of the Christian and cannot be renounced. To it is strictly bound the credibility of the proclamation about God that he or she must bring to today's world.

John Paul II reminded young people: "Pacifists, peacemakers—this is an exceptional category of persons whom Jesus calls blessed. The pleasure that our Lord takes in those who seek peace in family, social, work and political environments, at the national and international levels, is astonishingly contemporary.... To build the peace of today and of tomorrow, the peace of the year 2000—this is your task, if you want to call yourselves 'children of God.' Never forget that...peace and youth journey together."[50]

A call to open oneself without reserve

The prophet Isaiah continually returns to considerations of peace and commitments to peace on the part of all, not only the believing community. The Lord "shall judge between the nations, and shall decide for many peoples; and they shall beat their swords into plowshares, and their spears into pruning hooks; nation shall not lift up sword against nation, neither shall they learn war any more" (Is 2:4).

All this was to become reality when "there shall come forth a shoot from the stump of Jesse." With the Spirit of the Lord resting on him, "he shall not judge by what his eyes see, or decide by what his ears hear; but with righteousness he shall judge the poor, and decide with equity for the meek of the earth; and he shall smite the earth with the rod of his mouth, and with the breath of his lips he shall slay the wicked." It follows that men "shall not hurt or destroy in all my holy mountain; for the earth shall be full of the knowledge of the Lord as the waters cover the sea" (Is 11:1, 3-4, 9).

Peace is the gift of the risen Christ: "Peace be with you. As the Father has sent me, even so I send you" (Jn 20:21). Already at the moment of his birth he was announced as the bearer of definitive peace: "Glory to God in the highest, and on earth peace among men with whom he is pleased" (Lk 2:14; cf. 1:79). With his death and resurrection, he became for "our peace" forever (cf. Eph 3:14).

Reconciliation and communion with God are clearly fundamental elements of the peace that Christ gives us. But peace also signifies healing all other ruptures and contestations in our history that are derived from the rejection of God. It is pardon, reconciliation and renewal at the familial and social levels as well.

The certainty of the gift spurs the believer to make a courageous commitment. The profound preoccupation of his or her life is, as the Apostle Paul writes, "the equipment of the gospel of peace" (Eph 6:15). Continuing the mission of Christ, the Christian must also remain faithful to Christ's style, even among misunderstandings and rejections: "Whatever house you enter, first say, 'Peace be to this house!' And if a son of peace is there, your peace shall rest upon him; but if not, it shall return to you" (Lk 10:5-6).

But "peace at all times in all ways" (2 Thess 3:16) must not be regarded as a balance made of accommodations and of compromises: "Do you think that I have come to give peace on earth? No, I tell you, but rather division" (Lk 12:51). The perspective is not any peace whatsoever, but peace that bears a human quality—that is permeated by the values of liberty, justice and fraternity. Above all, the peace that tends to restore itself in humanity by virtue of the gift of Christ cannot be the fruit of fear or of the arrogance of the powerful. Instead, it will be the definitive conquest of these, as Mary sang in the *Magnificat*: "He has shown strength with his arm, he has scattered the proud in the imagination of their hearts, he has put down the mighty from their thrones, and exalted those of low degree" (Lk 1:51-52).

The Christian community is called to discern which peace proposals are truly worthy of human persons.

Mentality and culture of peace

"Peace is not merely the absence of war; nor can it be reduced solely to the maintenance of a balance of power between enemies; nor is it brought about by dictatorship. Instead, it is rightly and appropriately called an enterprise of justice. Peace results from that order structured into human society by its divine Founder, and actualized by men as they thirst after ever greater justice. The common good of humanity finds its ultimate meaning in the eternal law. But since the concrete demands of this common good are constantly changing as time goes on, peace is never attained once and for all, but must be built up ceaselessly."[51]

To enter into this dynamic vision of peace, we must eradicate from our hearts the "desires of the flesh," as the Apostle Paul says—that is, the "old man," prisoner of egoism and of stingy and self-interested calculations. Instead, it is necessary to affirm the "desires of the Spirit," characterized by fraternity and justice (cf. Gal 5:16-23).

What is at issue is not an alienating spiritualism, but the eradication of the ultimate root of all constestation and abuse of power. When our heart truly matures as the heart of a neighbor toward all, setting aside discrimination and prejudice, then freedom will no longer lead us to "bite and devour one another," but to rather place ourselves at the service of one another in charity (cf. Gal 5:13-15). Good does not become increasingly restricted within the close confines of individual advantage, but takes on the horizons of solidarity (cf. 1 Cor 10:23-25). Herein lies the secret of effective and lasting action for peace. Promotion of a mentality and culture of peace has become more indispensable today than ever.

To be set aside decisively are lifestyles and visions that are marked by contestation, especially if violent. When others don't think or act as we do, their positions can't be rejected a priori. Rather, we must see whether these might constitute an enrichment and development of what we have already discovered as true or just. The leavening of all sectors with the mentality and culture of reciprocity, of dialogue and of solidarity constitutes a priority objective for anyone who is sincerely seeking peace.

Horizons

The horizons of the commitment to peace must open us to the whole world. Otherwise, every project becomes unproductive and unrealistic. Already back in 1967, Paul VI wrote: "Excessive economic, social and cultural inequalities among peoples arouse tensions and conflicts, and are a danger to peace.... To wage war on misery and to struggle against injustice is to promote, along with improved conditions, the human and spiritual progress of all men, and therefore the common good of humanity."[52]

Developments in the eighties and early nineties eloquently confirm these affirmations. After the events of 1989 changed the face of Europe and of the world, we have become more clearly aware that the strongest threats to peace derive from the deep-rooted imbalance between the world's north and south.

This is the reason for the strong appeal that John Paul II has been making. He recalls first of all: "Just as the time has finally come when in individual states a system of private vendetta and reprisal has given way to the rule of law, so too a similar step forward is now urgently needed in the international community." And further: "For this reason, another name for peace is development. Just as there is a collective responsibility for avoiding war, so too there is a collective responsibility for promoting development. Just as within individual societies it is possible and right to organize a solid economy which will direct the functioning of the market to the common good, so too there is a similar need for adequate interventions on the international level." It becomes impossible to delay "a concerted worldwide effort to promote development, an effort which also involves sacrificing the positions of income and of power enjoyed by the more developed economies."[53]

Interdependence at a global level is a fact which no one can deny. The way in which it is planned and actualized depends on the political responsibility of all. Today, anyone who wishes to be a peacemaker must so work that present reality, characterized by opposition between the overdeveloped and the underdeveloped, will be replaced by a reality marked by true solidarity. For the believer, this must mean a solidarity open to the "specifically Christian dimension of total gratuity, forgiveness and reconciliation.... Awareness of the common fatherhood of God, of the brotherhood of all in Christ—'children in the Son'—and of the presence and life-giving action of the Holy Spirit will bring to our vision of the world a new criterion for interpreting it. Beyond human and natural bonds, already so close and strong, there is discerned in the light of faith a new model of the unity of the human race, which must ultimately inspire our solidarity."[54]

In this global context a space must be found for commitment to ecology. In the message for the 1990 Day of Peace, John Paul II emphasized: "Not a few ethical values, of fundamental importance for the development of a peaceful society, have a direct relationship with the question of the environment. The interdependence of many challenges which today's world must face confirms the urgency of interconnected solutions, based on a coherent moral vision of the world."

Of themselves the indispensable political and economic decisions are insufficient. First there must be a sincere conversion from lifestyles marked by consumerism. These are at the root of the new forms of alienation, which make the search for authentic peace more difficult."[55]

Commitment to peace is centered on respect for and sincere promotion of the personal dignity proper to every human being. Therefore, it requires that we begin by affirming that dignity in ourselves. Only in this way will we clearly be recognized as children of God.

For Reflection

There is real danger of reducing peace to a balance achieved through compromises. Sometimes even in daily life, it seems that truth and justice do nothing but create further tensions. Yet notwithstanding everything, they are indispensable to authentic peace. All this is made more urgent today by the possibility of creating and dissolving consensus.

Faith requires a decisive choice for peace but does not immediately point out the concrete steps to be taken for its true construction. These steps need to be identified by reading reality in the light of the Gospel. But it isn't always possible to reach practical conclusions, given the complexity of situations. Instead of opposing one another in the name of peace, why don't we put into effect the true pedagogy of communion that we desire: "together in thinking, together in planning, together in carrying the burden of commitments assumed, together...together"? Let's force ourselves to name the obstacles that hinder us from being together.

The promotion of a culture of peace is a priority. It calls for an attentive reading of the most varied cultural models in our society, contesting their factors of violence and of opposition and empowering persons who can bring about a true peace. Unless such work is done, the words of the Gospel about peace will remain too distant from concrete reality.

Blessed Are the Persecuted

Matthew presents the last beatitude in a more developed manner than the others. The passage does not limit itself to recalling that those persecuted for justice are blessed "for theirs is the kingdom of heaven," but specifies further: "Blessed are you when men revile you and persecute you and utter all kinds of evil against you falsely on my account. Rejoice and be glad, for your reward is great in heaven, for so men persecuted the prophets who were before you" (Mt 5:10-12; cf. Lk 6:22-23).

The justice referred to in this passage is that for which the blessed hunger and thirst. But what is chiefly stressed here is the strict connection of justice with Christ: to be persecuted for justice is the same as to be persecuted for Christ and vice-versa.

Against this background we can catch a glimpse of the situation of the primitive Christian community, which had quickly become the object of persecution. But we can also see a reality valid for all times: the incomprehension of the darkness in regard to the light does not limit itself to refuting the light, but almost always takes the form of struggle described thus: "If the world hates you, know that it has hated me before it hated you. If you were of the world, the world would love its own; but because you are not of the world, but I chose you out of the world, therefore the world hates you" (Jn 15:18-19).

Strengthened by the word of the Lord, the apostles who had been imprisoned and beaten, "left the presence of the council, rejoicing that they were counted worthy to suffer dishonor for the name. And every day in the temple and at home they did not cease teaching and preaching Jesus as the Christ" (Acts 5:41-42).

The same joy and courage characterized the successive journey of the Christian community: "Remember the word that I said to you, 'A servant is not greater than his master.' If they persecuted me, they will persecute you" (Jn 15:20). The many martyrs who proclaim the propagation of the faith are eloquent proof of this.

John Paul II reminds young adults: "Do not fear the exacting obligations that the beatitudes propose for the journey of your freedom. Do not become frightened by the lack of understanding that gospel fidelity can create around you: Christ calls you 'happy' even in persecutions suffered for him. Don't let yourselves be discouraged by the insufficiency of your strength and by the uncertainties that still mark your life in formation. The Spirit, who is the light and power of God, has been poured out into your hearts. He is capable of realizing great things in your docile availability."[56]

The courage of witness

Our local social context is distant from the situations in which religious liberty is denied and the faith constantly combated with every means, including violence. However, we have our own problems. The context of indifferentism and relativism in which we live can make our witness to the Gospel quite difficult.

Too often, adherence to our conscience becomes a source of alienation and loneliness. And this is especially true in certain professional sectors. All affirm the need for a mature and responsible conscience, but when we try to move from words to actions, by witnessing to the faith and committing ourselves to justice, we always bring on ourselves incomprehension and persecutions, more or less veiled.

Despite all this, or rather precisely because of all this, adherence to one's own conscience in professional practice is more urgent today.

To single out concrete forms of action, we will need to learn how to combine announcement of the truth with dialogue, courageous proposals with respectful listening, values that are open to ideals with the demands of concrete situations. In this regard, too, we will need to recall always that the Christian life is a journey toward the good and the true, along which we proceed only through stages that are sometimes very humble.

Not to be forgotten are the difficulties that the witness of Christian charity encounters in political life. Customs need to be overturned, such as blackmail and compromise. The moral question "shows the necessity that those who have the responsibility of guiding by whatever right, give witness first of all with their own life and with the way they exercise their office, to those superior values that are the foundation of civil community. But this also involves (and not as a simple spectator) every citizen who, with his or her conduct at work, in business, in family life, and in the exercise of political rights and duties, contributes to making the climate of his or her own environment and of the whole nation more or less sound and healthy. (*Evangelizzazione e testimonianza della carita,* [52]).

Equally difficult is witness in the economic field at all levels. When we don't follow the style of being shrewd, of exploiting, of aiming primarily at personal profit, we risk appearing stupid.

Together in the strength of the Spirit

The difficulties that announcing and witnessing to the Gospel and to justice continuously encounter must make us feel more strongly the need to travel together and sustain one another.

Even if traveling with others isn't always comfort-

able, because of objective factors that cannot quickly be overcome, we must always tend to root our witness in the community. Only by helping one another can each of us adhere to his or her conscience today. On the other hand, every time a believer is obliged to face the consequences of his or her witness, the community must never leave him or her alone. If we do so, we must reprove ourselves for a grave sin against charity and justice.

Not only the human value of solidarity is at stake, but faith in the promise of Christ: "For where two or three are gathered in my name, there am I in the midst of them" (Mt 18:20). These words refer directly to prayer, but it is not improper to read them in the perspective of the obligation to witness. In addition, this postulates that profound attitude of prayer which permits a real experience of the presence of him who has promised: "And lo, I am with you always, to the close of the age" (Mt 28:20).

Perhaps we give little thought to this need for prayer, especially when we are living the responsibility of every day. Yet the words of Christ are clear: "I am the vine, you are the branches. He who abides in me, and I in him, he it is that bears much fruit, for apart from me you can do nothing" (Jn 15:5). Therefore, it is necessary to pray always and not lose heart (cf. Lk 18:1).

When we pray, especially when we pray together, we can relive the joyous experience of Pentecost. Fear of persecution is transformed into the courageous assurance of proclamation. Coming to assist our weakness, the Spirit makes "everything...work(s) for good with those who love him" (Rom 8:28).

The assurance of proclamation

Greater assurance in the proclamation of the Gospel becomes more urgent day by day. John Paul II continually appeals for a renewed commitment to the new evangelization on the part of the whole Christian community.

The evangelization referred to chooses the way of charity, sharing, above all, the expectations, sufferings and commitment to liberation of the poor and the oppressed. Therefore, an integral part of this way is a social proclamation for the promotion of justice, taking responsibility for "everything that is authentically human and more closely touches the person, the family and various community and social categories."[57]

But we must also learn to dialogue with the culture of our time. Otherwise, our language and emphasis could constitute an obstacle to encountering Christ.

Our gaze must embrace the whole world. A new missionary thrust is needed, for which the sensitivity and availability of young adults will be fundamental. It is necessary to proclaim to all people, writes John Paul II, that "true liberation consists in opening oneself to the love of Christ. In him, and only in him, are we set free from all alienation and doubt, from slavery to the power of sin and death. Christ is truly 'our peace' (Eph 2:14); 'the love of Christ impels us' (2 Cor 5:14), giving meaning and joy to our life. Mission is an issue of faith, an accurate indicator of our faith in Christ and his love for us."[58]

The way of the beatitudes flows into precisely these horizons, as wide as the whole world—a world that needs the proclamation of the Gospel not only for building itself in a manner respecting the dignity of each person, but above all in order to open itself to Christ, "the way, and the truth, and the life" (Jn 14:6), "the Alpha and the Omega, the first and the last, the beginning and the end" (Rev 22:13). We cannot halt in the commitment to evangelization because "there is no other name under heaven given among men by which we must be saved" (Acts 4:12).

For Reflection

In our society there is particular sensitivity to what others say about us. Often we sacrifice personal integrity and authenticity to an image; or else we change our ideas and positions not because we've discovered that they are false, but only because they aren't shared by others. But then what becomes of liberty, of conscience, of personal dignity? What qualities will tomorrow's society possess?

We are quick to cast stones at people who are inconsistent, forgetting that we ourselves are the same. To those who wanted to stone the woman caught in adultery, Christ said only: "Let him who is without sin among you be the first to throw a stone at her" (Jn 8:7). When we are ready to condemn others, what would happen if Christ repeated those same words to us? Must we not perhaps act like the accusers of the adulteress, who "went away, one by one, beginning with the eldest"? (Jn 8:9)

John Paul II has written this about missionary commitment: "I ask young people...to listen to Christ's words as he says to them what he once said to Simon Peter and to Andrew at the lakeside: 'Follow me, and I will make you fishers of men' (Mt 4:19). May they have the courage to reply as Isaiah did: 'Here I am, Lord! I am ready! Send me!' (cf. Is 6:8) They will have a wonderful life ahead of them, and they will know the genuine joy of proclaiming the 'Good News' to brothers and sisters whom they will lead on the way of salvation."[59] This perspective can be yours, through Christ's gift and your conscious response. If the gift is offered to you, become alert, make yourself worthy of it and accept it. "The harvest is great." Try to think about this.

LET'S CELEBRATE THE LORD OUR GOD

Praise with all creation

"Most High, Almighty, good Lord,
To you be praise, glory, and honor,
 and all blessings;
To you alone! Most High, do they belong,
And no man is worthy of speaking your name!

Be praised, Lord, with all your creatures,
And above all our Brother Sun,
Who gives us the day by which you light
 our way,
And who is beautiful, radiant, and with his great
 splendor
Is a symbol to us of you, O Most High!

And be praised, Lord, for Sister Moon
 and the Stars,
You created them in the heavens, bright,
 precious, and beautiful!

And be praised, Lord, for our Brother the Wind,
And for the air and clouds, and for fair weather
 and all other,
Through which you sustain your creatures.

And be praised, Lord, for our Sister Water,
So useful, and humble, and chaste!

And be praised, Lord, for our Brother Fire,
Through whom you light up the night:
And who is handsome, joyful, robust, and
 strong!

And be praised, my Lord, for our Sister,
   Mother Earth,
Who supports and carries us,
And produces the diverse fruits and colorful
   flowers and the trees!

Be blessed, Lord, for all who, for your sake,
   forgive their enemies,
And have to suffer injustice and tribulation;

And blessed are those who persevere in peace,
For they will be rewarded by you, Most High!

Be praised, my Lord, for our Sister,
   bodily Death,
From whom no living man can escape!
Woe only to those who die in mortal sin;

But blessed are those who have done your most
   holy will;
For the second death can cause them no harm!

Praise and bless the Lord and give thanks to him
And serve him with great humility!"

   —*St. Francis of Assisi* [60]

Witness

The Message of Francis of Assisi

As a conclusion of our reflections on the beatitudes, I invite you to listen briefly to Francis of Assisi. We will draw directly from his writings. For centuries, his life and message have stimulated generations of believers to say a more radical and ready "yes" to the logic of the beatitudes. Even to us today, his example speaks in strong terms.

The beatitudes

Here is the synthesis of the beatitudes which Francis proposed for himself and others:

"Blessed are the poor in spirit, for theirs is the kingdom of heaven.

There are many people who work hard at prayer and their duties; making many sacrifices and bodily mortifications; but for just one word that might be a personal insult, or because something or other has been taken from them, they are scandalized and immediately become irritated or angry.

These are not poor in spirit, because one who is truly poor in spirit detests himself and loves those who slap his face.

Blessed are the peacemakers, for they shall be called sons of God.

The true peacemakers are those who for love of our Lord Jesus Christ conserve their peace of soul and body amid all the things that they endure in this world.

Blessed are the pure of heart, for they shall see God.

The pure of heart are those who despise earthly

things and seek the heavenly. They never cease to adore and to view the living and true Lord God with their pure heart and soul.

Blessed is that servant who does not pride himself more on the good that the Lord says and does through him, than on that which the Lord works through others. The person sins who wants to receive from his neighbor more than what he wants to give of himself to the Lord God.

Blessed is the person who sustains his neighbor in his weakness as he would wish to be sustained himself in a similar case.

Blessed is the servant who gives all his goods to the Lord God; someone who keeps things for himself hides the talent given by the Lord, and what he thinks he has will be taken away.

Blessed is the servant who does not think himself better when he is honored and exalted by men than when he is regarded as vile, naive and despicable, for man possesses the value he has before God and nothing more....

Blessed is that religious who takes joy and gladness nowhere else than in the most holy words and deeds of the Lord and through these leads men to love God in joy and gladness.

Blessed is that servant who loves the brother who is ill and cannot repay him, more than he loves the healthy person who can compensate him.

Blessed is that servant who can love and fear his brother when he is far away as if he were near, and will say nothing behind his back that with charity he would not say to his face."[61]

If we open ourselves to the beatitudes, allowing ourselves to affirm them in our life, we will drive away evil and fear:

"Where there are love and wisdom,
there is no fear nor ignorance.
Where there are patience and humility,
there is no anger nor disturbance.
Where there is joyful poverty,
there is no greed nor avarice.
Where there are quiet and meditation,
there is neither preoccupation nor dissipation.
Where there is fear of the Lord to guard the house,
there is no enemy who can manage to enter.
Where there are mercy and discretion,
there is neither pride nor harshness."[62]

True happiness

One day, near the church of St. Mary of the Angels, Francis spoke to Brother Leo about true joy:

"Returning from Perugia in the middle of the night, I get this far and it's winter, muddy and so cold that my habit is covered from top to bottom with ice which bangs continually on my legs until they bleed from the wounds. I'm all muddy, cold and icy. I reach the door, and after I've knocked and called out for a long time, a brother comes and asks: "Who is it?"

I reply: "Brother Francis."

And he says: "Go away! It isn't a decent hour to arrive. You can't come in."

Then when I insist, he replies: "Go away, you're a simpleton and an idiot who can't come here now; there are many of us and we don't need you!"

And I still stay in front of the door and plead: "For love of God, welcome me for tonight."

And he replies: "I won't do it! Go to the Crociferi (the hospital) and ask them."

Well, if I have patience and don't become upset, I

tell you that here are true joy and true virtue and salvation of soul."[63]

Prayer

Prayer is indispensable for living in perfect joy. This is the way Francis personalized the prayer which Christ had taught to his disciples:

"Our *most holy* Father: *Creator, Redeemer, Consoler and our Savior.*

Who art in heaven: *in the angels and in the saints, illuminating them to know that you, Lord, are light; inflaming them to love, because you, Lord, are love; living in them, fullness of their joy, because you, Lord, are the greatest good, eternal, from whom comes all good, without whom there is no good.*

Hallowed be your name: *may knowledge of you be clearer in us, so we can see the breadth of your good* deeds, the extent of your promises, the heights of your majesty, the depths of your judgments.

Your kingdom come: *so that you may reign in us by means of grace and make us reach your kingdom, where there is vision of you without shadow, perfect love, happy union, enjoyment without end.*

May your will be done on earth as it is in heaven: *so that we may love you with all our heart, always thinking of you; with all our soul, always desiring you; with all our mind, directing all our intentions toward you and looking for your honor in everything. And with all our strength, spending all our energies and sensibilities of soul and body in the service of your love and for nothing else; and so that we may love our neighbor as ourselves, with all our power drawing everyone to love you, rejoicing in the good of others as in our own, sympathizing with their problems and offending no one.*

Give us this day our daily bread: *give us today your beloved Son, our Lord Jesus Christ: that we may remember and reverently understand the love that he had for us and everything that he said, did and suffered for us.*

And forgive us our trespasses: *through your indescribable mercy, in virtue of the passion of your Son and through the intercession and merits of the most holy Virgin Mary and of all your saints.*

As we forgive those who trespass against us: *and whomever we cannot fully forgive, may you, Lord, enable us to pardon fully, that through your love we can truly love our enemies and devoutly intercede for them before you, and render evil for evil to no one, and seek to be helpful to everyone in you.*

And lead us not into temptation: *hidden or manifest, sudden or persistent.*

But deliver us from evil: *past, present and future.* Amen."[64]

Notes

1. John Paul II. "To the Youth of Europe," in *La Traccia*, 10 (1988), pp. 1935-36.

2. Dupont, J. "Beatitudine/Beatitudini," in *Nuovo dizionario teologia biblica*. Milan: Edizioni Paoline, 1988, p. 158.

3. *Ibid.*, p. 159.

4. Vatican Council II. *Pastoral Constitution on the Church in the Modern World (Gaudium et Spes)*. Boston: St. Paul Books & Media (Pauline Books & Media), 1966, n. 16.

5. John Paul II. *The Role of the Christian Family in the Modern World (Familiaris Consortio)*. Boston: St. Paul Books & Media (Pauline Books & Media), 1981, n. 34.

6. Cf. Vatican Council II. *Dogmatic Constitution on the Church (Lumen Gentium)*. Boston: St. Paul Books & Media (Pauline Books & Media), 1966, n. 41.

7. Vatican Council II. *Pastoral Constitution on the Church in the Modern World, op. cit.*, n. 17.

8. John Paul II. *On Human Work (Laborem Exercens)*. Boston: St. Paul Books & Media (Pauline Books & Media), 1981, n. 14.

9. John Paul II. *On Social Concern (Sollicitudo Rei Socialis)*. Boston: St. Paul Books & Media (Pauline Books & Media), 1988, n. 28.

10. John Paul II. *Mother of the Redeemer (Redemptoris Mater)*. Boston: St. Paul Books & Media (Pauline Books & Media), 1987, n. 37.

11. John Paul II. *On the Hundredth Anniversary of Rerum Novarum (Centesimus Annus)*. Boston: St. Paul Books & Media (Pauline Books & Media), 1991, n. 35.

12. John Paul II. *The Redeemer of Man (Redemptor Hominis)*. Boston: St. Paul Books & Media (Pauline Books & Media), 1979, n. 15.

13. John Paul II. *On the Hundredth Anniversary of Rerum Novarum, op. cit.*, n. 36.

14. Vatican Council II. *Pastoral Constitution on the Church in the Modern World, op. cit.,* n. 21.

15. John Paul II. *Insegnamenti di Giovanni Paolo II,* vol. 8/1. Vatican Press, 1986, pp. 358-59.

16. Augustine, St. *Confessions,* book 1, 1.

17. *Ibid.,* book 10, 27.

18. Vatican Council II. *Pastoral Constitution on the Church in the Modern World, op. cit.,* n. 17.

19. John Paul II. *On the Christian Meaning of Human Suffering (Salvifici Doloris).* Boston: St. Paul Books & Media (Pauline Books & Media), 1984, n. 3.

20. *Ibid.,* n. 26.

21. *Ibid.,* n. 19.

22. Bauder, W. "Umilta', mansuetudine," in *Dizionario dei concetti biblici del Nuovo Testamento.* Bologna: AA.VV., 1976, p. 1905.

23. Vatican Council II. *Declaration on Religious Freedom (Dignitatis Humanae).* Boston: St. Paul Books & Media (Pauline Books & Media), 1966, n. 1.

24. Synod on the Laity. *Concluding Message,* 1987, n. 3.

25. Vatican Council II. *Pastoral Constitution on the Church in the Modern World, op. cit.,* n. 21.

26. John Paul II. *Insegnamenti di Giovanni Paolo II,* vol. 8/1, *op. cit.,* p. 361.

27. John Paul II. *On Social Concern, op. cit.,* n. 41.

28. *Ibid.*

29. Cf. Vatican Council II. *Pastoral Constitution on the Church in the Modern World, op. cit.,* n. 43.

30. *Ibid.,* n. 74.

31. John Paul II. *The Lay Members of Christ's Faithful People (Christifideles Laici).*

32. *Ibid.*

33. Vatican Council II. *Pastoral Constitution on the Church in the Modern World, op. cit.,* n. 75.

34. Paul VI. *The Coming Eightieth (Octagesima Adveniens).* Boston: St. Paul Books & Media (Pauline Books & Media), 1971, n. 4.

35. Vatican Council II. *Pastoral Constitution on the Church in the Modern World, op. cit.,* n. 43.

36. Synod on the Laity. *Final Proposals,* 1987, n. 5.

37. John Paul II. *On the Mercy of God (Dives in Misericordia).* Boston: St. Paul Books & Media (Pauline Books & Media), 1980, n. 2.

38. John Paul II. *Insegnamenti di Giovanni Paolo II,* vol. 8/1, *op. cit.,* pp. 359-60.

39. John Paul II. *On the Mercy of God, op. cit.,* n. 4.

40. Tannoia, A. *Vita,* vol. I. Naples: 1798, pp. 152-53.

41. John Paul II. *On the Mercy of God, op. cit.,* n. 3.

42. Link, H.G. and J. Scnnemann. "Puro," in *Dizionario dei concetti biblici del Nuovo Testamento, op. cit.,* p. 1487.

43. Liguori, St. Alphonsus. *Opere ascetiche,* 10. Rome: Editrice di Storia e Letteratura, 1968, pp. 315-16.

44. Augustine, St. *Confessions,* book 13: 9-10.

45. C.E.I. *Evangelizzazione e testimonianza della caritá,* 22.

46. *Ibid.*

47. John Paul II. *On the Hundredth Anniversary of Rerum Novarum, op. cit.,* n. 36.

48. John Paul II. *Insegnamenti di Giovanni Paolo II,* vol. 8/1, *op. cit.,* p. 359.

49. Vatican Council II. *Pastoral Constitution on the Church in the Modern World, op. cit.,* n. 77.

50. John Paul II. *Insegnamenti di Giovanni Paolo II,* vol. 8/1, *op. cit.,* p. 360.

51. Vatican Council II. *Pastoral Constitution on the Church in the Modern World, op. cit.,* n. 78.

52. Paul VI. *On the Development of Peoples (Populorum Progressio).* Boston: St. Paul Books & Media (Pauline Books & Media), 1967, n. 76.

53. John Paul II. *On the Hundredth Anniversary of Rerum Novarum, op. cit.,* n. 52.

54. John Paul II. *On Social Concern, op. cit.,* n. 40.

55. John Paul II. *On the Hundredth Anniversary of Rerum Novarum, op. cit.,* n. 41.

56. John Paul II. *Insegnamenti di Giovanni Paolo II,* vol. 8/1, *op. cit.,* p. 966.

57. C.E.I. *Evangelizzazione e testimonianza della caritá, op. cit.,* 7.

58. John Paul II. *The Mission of the Redeemer (Redemptoris Missio).* Boston: St. Paul Books & Media (Pauline Books & Media), 1991, n. 11.

59. *Ibid.,* n. 80.

60. Cristiani, L. *Saint Francis of Assisi.* Boston: St. Paul Books & Media (Pauline Books & Media),, 1983, pp. 143-44, 161-62.

61. *Fonte francescane.* Padua: 1982, pp. 143-47.

62. *Ibid.,* p. 147.

63. *Ibid.,* p. 183.

64 *Ibid.,* p. 180-81.

About the Author

Sabatino Majorano, C.Ss.R., is a professor of moral theology at the Alfonsian Academy of the Pontifical Lateran University. He has published various studies on moral, spiritual and catechetical topics.

About the Series

These booklets are intended to help today's young (and not-so-young) adult explore how the ten commandments and eight beatitudes relate to human life and divine realities: How and where do they fit into contemporary culture and God's plan for us? The editors hope that *Reflections on the Commandments* and *Beatitudes* will stimulate both deeper reflection and further research.

Booklets in this series: I Am the Lord Your God; You Shall Not Have Strange Gods Before Me; You Shall Not Take the Lord's Name in Vain; Remember to Keep Holy the Lord's Day; Honor Your Father and Your Mother; You Shall Not Kill; You Shall Not Commit Adultery, Nor Covet Your Neighbor's Wife; You Shall Not Steal, Nor Covet Your Neighbor's Goods; You Shall Not Bear False Witness; Blessed Are the Poor in Spirit.

St. Paul Book & Media Centers

ALASKA
750 West 5th Ave., Anchorage, AK 99501; 907-272-8183
CALIFORNIA
3908 Sepulveda Blvd., Culver City, CA 90230; 310-397-8676
5945 Balboa Ave., San Diego, CA 92111; 619-565-9181
46 Geary Street, San Francisco, CA 94108; 415-781-5180
FLORIDA
145 S.W. 107th Ave., Miami, FL 33174; 305-559-6715
HAWAII
1143 Bishop Street, Honolulu, HI 96813; 808-521-2731
ILLINOIS
172 North Michigan Ave., Chicago, IL 60601; 312-346-4228
LOUISIANA
4403 Veterans Memorial Blvd., Metairie, LA 70006; 504-887-7631
MASSACHUSETTS
50 St. Paul's Ave., Jamaica Plain, Boston, MA 02130; 617-522-8911
Rte. 1, 885 Providence Hwy., Dedham, MA 02026; 617-326-5385
MISSOURI
9804 Watson Rd., St. Louis, MO 63126; 314-965-3512
NEW JERSEY
561 U.S. Route 1, Wick Plaza, Edison, NJ 08817; 908-572-1200
NEW YORK
150 East 52nd Street, New York, NY 10022; 212-754-1110
78 Fort Place, Staten Island, NY 10301; 718-447-5071
OHIO
2105 Ontario Street, Cleveland, OH 44115; 216-621-9427
PENNSYLVANIA
510 Holstein Street, Bridgeport, PA 19405; 610-277-7728
SOUTH CAROLINA
243 King Street, Charleston, SC 29401; 803-577-0175
TENNESSEE
4811 Poplar Ave., Memphis, TN 38117; 901-761-2987
TEXAS
114 Main Plaza, San Antonio, TX 78205; 210-224-8101
VIRGINIA
1025 King Street, Alexandria, VA 22314; 703-549-3806
GUAM
285 Farenholt Ave., Suite 308, Tamuning, Guam 96911; 671-649-4377
CANADA
3022 Dufferin Street, Toronto, Ontario, Canada M6B 3T5; 416-781-9131